363
Q

Quarles, John R.

Cleaning up America

333

DATE			

CLEANING UP AMERICA

An Insider's View of the
Environmental Protection Agency

CLEANING UP
AMERICA

An Insider's View of the
Environmental Protection Agency

JOHN QUARLES

Illustrated with photographs

HOUGHTON MIFFLIN COMPANY BOSTON

1976

Library of Congress Cataloging in Publication Data

Quarles, John R
   Cleaning up America.

   Includes index.
   1. United States. Environmental Protection Agency.
I. Title.
TD171.Q3   363   76-25420
ISBN 0-395-24772-1

Printed in the United States of America
C 10 9 8 7 6 5 4 3 2 1

To Barbara ,
with love

Acknowledgments

SINCE I HAVE WRITTEN this book during my tenure as Deputy Administrator of the Environmental Protection Agency, it needs to be said that I have written it entirely by myself, working through draft after draft on Saturdays and Sundays and late into the night, on airplanes and in airports and in hotels, from Nome, Alaska, to Mexico City and Brazil. Though the book reveals my experience as a government official, it is a personal account. The views expressed are my own, and they are not offered in any sense in my official capacity.

Yet no man works alone. I have received help from many good friends who read drafts of the manuscript and gave me their criticism and suggestions. They include Michael Frome, Frederick Anderson, Joan and Alan Kirk, Lorna and John Flynn, Michele Frome, and Roger Williams. I am especially indebted to Robert Rauch for his extensive comments and to Dorothy Reister for her constant encouragement.

Most of all I am indebted to my wife, Barbara, whose support has known no limits. I also express thanks to my children, Laura, Nancy, and Jack; they did not share in the decision to undertake this effort, but, like Barbara, they have shared in the personal sacrifice it has required.

Contents

Illustrations

(following page 120)

The other side of the Statue of Liberty. *EPA-Documerica — Gary Miller*

Closed beach, Lake Erie. *EPA-Documerica — Frank Aleksandrowicz*

Fishkill, Hudson River. *Photo by M. Dixson, Courtesy New York State Health Department*

"Dredge and fill" development, Marco Island, Florida. *EPA-Documerica — Flip Schulke*

Rush hour, Southeast Freeway in Houston. *EPA-Documerica — Blair Pittman*

Dumping waste in Lake Superior

Walter J. Hickel

William Ruckelshaus. *EPA*

Ruckelshaus, with Russell Train and John Quarles. *EPA*

Smog over Birmingham, Alabama, Novenber 1971. *Birmingham News*

The U.S. Steel plant at Birmingham. *Birmingham* News

The Florida Power and Light plant at Turkey Point, Florida, before and after the building of canals to cool and recycle hot water. *Courtesy Florida Power and Light Company*

Introduction

I AM a federal bureaucrat. I am one of those bureaucrats everyone complains of, the ones who frustrate worthy government programs and tangle them in endless red tape. I am part of the faceless, gray government machine. I am one of those government officials whom cartoonists make fun of and editorialists stick pins in, who are blasted with criticism by public leaders from Barry Goldwater to Ralph Nader. I am one of those whom George Wallace has called lazy, incompetent, and "pointy-headed . . . who probably carry peanut butter sandwiches to work in brown bags." Yes, I am a bureaucrat.

The criticisms are largely based on ignorance. Unless they have actually worked in government, few people have any idea what life in the bureaucracy is really like. I'd like to set a few facts straight. For one thing, I do not eat peanut butter sandwiches.

I am also an environmentalist, a chief official of the United States Environmental Protection Agency since its creation in December 1970, and in that capacity, too, I have been the object of heated criticism. The agency has been the target of the power industry, the steel industry, the auto industry, labor unions, farmers, editorialists, and private citizens. Its actions have been attacked as arbitrary, unreasonable, narrow-minded, impractical, and un-American. Again, much of this condemnation has frequently been based on misunderstanding.

The odd thing is that I never planned to be either a bureaucrat or an environmentalist. I planned to be a lawyer and live in Boston, where I grew up. In the fall of 1968 I was well started down that path. I had been practicing law for six years with one of Boston's leading law firms, and my wife, Barbara, and I were happily settled in one of the city's suburbs. Although I had always had an interest in government, I had no thought at all that within a few months I would disrupt my legal career, move my family to Washington, and plunge into the turbulent Washington life.

The events that caused this change started by happenstance. As I walked back to my office from lunch one day after Christmas, a newspaper headline caught my eye. It announced that Elliot Richardson had been named the new Under Secretary of State. Elliot Richardson and my father had been law partners, and I had talked to him about politics and public service when I was in high school. Suddenly an idea leaped into my mind. Was it possible that he might take me with him? I returned to my desk and impulsively called his office to request an interview.

When I was turned down by Richardson a few weeks later, my interest surely would have died, but by then events were running on a course of their own. I had discovered a friend who took over my cause. One of the older lawyers in the firm, Jack Weitzel, had worked in Washington throughout the Eisenhower years. When he heard I was seeking a government job, he joined my effort with an enthusiasm and tenacity that exceeded my own. Weitzel started sending letters, with copies of my résumé, to all his friends, pursuing any leads he had as each appointment in the new Republican administration was announced. At one point I almost landed a job with the Under Secretary of Housing and Urban Development. When that fell through I was ready to quit, but Jack Weitzel kept sending out his letters.

One Sunday afternoon in March I was out in our backyard

playing in the snow with our children, Laura and Nancy. Way above us, an upstairs window opened and Barbara called out, "John, you have a long-distance phone call. It's Russell Train." My heartbeat quickened. I had never heard of Russell Train until a few weeks before, when he was appointed Under Secretary of the Interior, but the next day I found myself on an airplane, flying to Washington for an interview. I entered the large Interior Department building, with its rows of corridors each a block long, and with a sense of exploring the unknown I walked down the hallway on the fifth floor to the impressively furnished office of the Under Secretary. I immediately liked Russ Train. He was relaxed and gracious in his manner, yet an air of excitement filled his office. He must have thought the interview went well; when it ended, he tentatively offered me a job.

The decision was not easy. With two young children and a third due soon, I wondered how wise it was to interrupt my legal career for the uncertainties of a staff position in the Department of the Interior. Despite my qualms, Barbara and I decided we should take our chances. In May 1969, three weeks after our son, Jack, was born, I entered a new world — the world of the bureaucracy.

I worked for Russ Train at Interior for six months and then for the next twelve months served as a close staff aide to the Secretary of the Interior, Walter J. Hickel. When I was about to leave the government, another event intervened. The U.S. Environmental Protection Agency was created in December 1970, and its first Administrator, William D. Ruckelshaus, asked me to join his new team. For the next two and a half years, I served as EPA's chief legal officer and also as its first Assistant Administrator for Enforcement. I was responsible for developing a program of aggressive enforcement of the existing environmental regulations. I was also in charge of creating a new regulatory program, which required every industry discharging pollutants into water to obtain a government permit and to abide by the controls it imposed. When Bill Ruckelshaus left EPA in mid-1973, the President named Russell Train as his successor. Once again I was working for the man who had brought me to Washington. Russ Train asked me to become Deputy Administrator of EPA, the number two position in the agency. Since then I have been totally engaged in the full range of EPA's programs and controversies.

The environmental movement has been one of America's most effective protests. It grew out of decades of abuse of our environment. It gained power from the rebellion of youth, which dominated the civil rights and antiwar movements of the 1960s. At its peak it attracted vocal support from nearly all groups within the nation. It became a crusade.

That crusade has produced momentous changes. It has caused the enactment of ambitious statutes, redirected major government programs, overturned established practices throughout American industry, and touched the daily lives of citizens everywhere — in the products we buy, the taxes we pay, the air we breathe, and the water we drink. One result of this protest movement was creation of the Environmental Protection Agency. With a total work force of ten thousand people, EPA operates a range of programs that includes research, technical analysis, standard-setting, and enforcement. EPA makes grants of roughly $100 million a year to a variety of state and local environmental agencies, and the EPA grants to build municipal sewage treatment plants are financing the biggest public works program in the country. The control of these programs and expenditures makes EPA one of the most powerful agencies in the United States government. It is the most important regulatory agency created since the New Deal.

Some have said EPA is too powerful. As Congressman Jamie L. Whitten, chairman of the House Appropriations subcommittee responsible for EPA, repeatedly warned Bill Ruckelshaus, "You have more power than a good man would want, or a bad man should have."

The job of cleaning up America means different things to different people. To me it chiefly has meant the mobilization of the powers of government to restrict abuse of our environment.

I have written this book about EPA from the inside, looking out. It is a candid, personal account of the turmoil I have lived through. I have described the people I have worked with and the troubles we have confronted. In writing these chapters I have relived my own experience, my feelings of excitement and satisfaction and of frustration and dismay.

The book consists of a series of separate episodes, each told in its own chronology and in full detail. In choosing this approach, I have not attempted to write a history of the environmental movement or to describe comprehensively our nation's environmental damage. Yet the collection of these episodes does indicate how our government responded to demands by people to do *something* about the abuse of the environment. The incidents show how decisions on critical environmental issues actually were made, and describe not only the achievements and the failures, but also the confusion, the pressures, and the distractions that beset top government officials.

The intensity of my experience has convinced me that our government is responsive and that, given adequate time, it can produce solutions to certain national problems. Great headway has been made in cleaning up glaring examples of air and water pollution. Despite that progress, many grave environmental problems are not yet being effectively addressed. These problems are, of course, the fodder of politics, and charges abound as to who is at fault. Beneath these attempts to place the blame, however, lies a problem that I have only slowly come to recognize, and the more I understand it, the more it worries me: since government action depends on public demand, the government does not begin to attack a problem until that problem has become severe. The government always has to catch up, to find solutions for problems that long before have grown out of control. Although our government may be responsive, it is so only by delayed reaction. The lag time between need and response is measured in years.

The pollution of our environment demonstrates how long it often takes before serious problems are recognized and attacked. The momentum of our economic growth makes that hiatus a potential danger. As the speed of our economy continues to accelerate, and as the resultant stresses upon our environment and our finite natural resources become increasingly complex, we are posed with a frightening question: Shall we always be able to afford that delay?

PART I

Protest
and Response

CHAPTER 1

Wally Hickel's Decision

TUESDAY, MAY 21, 1972, had been the type of day they advertise in southern Florida — sunny, bright, and delightfully warm — but as I looked through the helicopter windows I saw clouds gathering. A shower threatened. Above us the huge rotor blades of the helicopter beat the air incessantly, noisily. It was almost deafening.

I had flown to Miami from Washington at the end of the previous day, traveling with Alan Kirk, who was the Deputy General Counsel of the Environmental Protection Agency and, after our three years in the government together, one of my closest friends. We had arrived at dusk at the elegant Doral Hotel. Driving in past the manicured greens and fairways, Alan and I had marveled at the layout. "Do you have two full golf courses here?" I asked at the registration desk. "No," the desk clerk politely answered, "we have five." Such are the Florida cities that blossom out of the swamp.

In the morning I had given a speech to a conference of electric company executives, and then we had hopped aboard the waiting helicopter to visit the Turkey Point generating plant of the Florida Power and Light Company. That plant had caused one of the big early battles in the environmental rebellion, and we wanted to inspect the construction work being carried out by the company under the consent decree that had settled the case.

Despite the past antagonisms, the company officials re-

ceived us graciously. After a picnic lunch, they gave us a full
tour of the plant, even of the inside of the awesome concrete
shell housing the nuclear power unit, which was almost
completed. Finally we climbed back into the helicopter to fly
over the whole facility, including the network of cooling
canals being constructed under our consent decree to prevent discharges of hot water from destroying life in the
tropical waters of Biscayne Bay. Beneath us the landscape
spread in all directions, almost completely flat. To the east
we could look across Biscayne Bay to Elliott Key, eight or ten
miles away. Below and to the west as far as the eye could
see stretched the Florida everglades, a wetland wilderness whose low bushes and grasses were interspersed with
patches of open water.

My mind drifted back to another spring afternoon two
years before. I recalled a conversation with the man whose
decision to go to court had proved the turning point in the
tangled history of the Turkey Point dispute, the man who
was then my boss, Secretary of the Interior Walter J. Hickel.
I had been working with him alone in his office one day after
the suit was filed, and I asked him why he had done it.

"If you think it's easy to make these decisions," he said,
"you ought to sit up here and try to make them. They stick
with you — right or wrong." His outstretched arm had swept
through the air, then stopped and slammed down on the glass
that covered his desk. His voice had boomed forth, filling the
vast spaciousness of his high-ceilinged, wood-paneled office.
Seated calmly on one of the blue leather chairs just ten
or fifteen feet away, I was struck by the tension in his
voice.

Hickel abruptly bounded up from his high-backed swivel
chair and paced toward the windows at the side of the room.
He stopped and spun about to face me. His solid frame and
trim figure gave a sense of physical power, and the spring in
his step showed he was still in good condition. As he talked,

his dark eyes flashed with enthusiasm and his face lit up. He had the direct and simple assertiveness that had brought him success on the Alaskan frontier. Wally Hickel viewed life as a battle, and with a cocky self-assurance and an occasional bit of bravado he was always ready to plunge into a fight. Yet he knew that in politics, especially in Washington, one pays dearly for one's mistakes. On that afternoon his words broke the tranquillity of the sunshine flooding into his office through the large windows and bounced against the distant wall at the other end of the room. He paused, then spoke out again, this time a bit more softly. "I can tell you when I made that decision," he said firmly. "I was sitting in my car in the basement of this building, and I suddenly said to myself, 'I'll do it!'"

And yet, I wondered, why did he do it? Why did Hickel start the law suit against Florida Power and Light?

That question rattled around in my mind as I looked out across the everglades. We had flown slowly over the whole area of construction work, including the full length of the six-mile canal, which would carry hot water away from Biscayne Bay and empty it into Card Sound until the entire recycling system was finished. The small helicopter was able to carry only four of us. The pilot and I had the seats in front, where the clear plastic shell gave us a view — right down to our feet. Behind us were Kirk and a representative of the company. The helicopter stopped moving forward and slowly descended until it came to rest on a small patch of ground outside the diked area. Raindrops splashed around us, but we could see a well, dug below the surface, where the quality of the water in the porous limestone underlying the area was being monitored. After briefly examining the well, we lifted off again and continued our inspection flight.

The roar of the helicopter's rotor discouraged frivolous talk and left me free to let my own thoughts run. I glanced back at Alan Kirk and thought it was fitting that he and I were making this trip together. Both of us had been working on Hickel's personal staff when he had initiated the law suit. That was early in 1970, before Hickel was fired by President Nixon and before EPA was even formed. A lot had happened in the meantime, but this case stood out as one of the biggest contests we had fought. I had put a lot of emotion into the effort against the company, but I had never had a chance to see firsthand what we had been fighting over. It was exciting to go there now, after the consent decree had been signed, and see the abatement system actually being constructed. It gave me a sense of achievement — a satisfaction that anyone working in Washington often sorely needs.

It had started as a textbook case of environmental mismanagement. To meet its soaring demands for electricity, Florida Power and Light had begun, years before, to build a massive generating complex at Turkey Point on the southeastern coast, twenty-five miles below Miami. The catch was that the generating units would require huge amounts of cooling water to condense the steam used to drive the turbines, and that water, after being superheated, would be discharged into Biscayne Bay. The bay was a shallow tropical estuary, with a rich aquatic life that was both precious and fragile. Biscayne Bay had just been declared a national monument, part of the National Parks system, because so many other areas with a similar ecosystem had already been wiped out. Environmentalists had pointed out that the gushing flow of hot water from the power plant — "thermal pollution" — would devastate marine life in sizable portions of Biscayne Bay.

By 1969, protests against the Turkey Point plant were creating sharp controversy. Nathaniel Reed, the youthful, aggressive head of the Florida state pollution control agency, and citizen environmentalists were building pressure against the project. The company, which had already invested millions of dollars, was forging ahead with its plans. The two sides were heading for a showdown. In December, Florida Governor Claude Kirk — no relation to Alan — requested support from Secretary Hickel, and in February a federal-state enforcement conference was held to discuss the problem. When the company rejected the recommendations of the participants in that conference, the question was referred back to Wally Hickel. Would he take up the battle? It was indeed a hot issue for him, rife with political risks. He responded by bringing suit to block the company's plans.

The significance of Hickel's decision to sue the Florida Power and Light Company in March of 1970 lay only partly in the ecological values at stake in Biscayne Bay. They were important, but were completely overshadowed by another fact: this was the first time that any Secretary of the Interior had *ever* brought suit against a company to challenge its operations because of their effect on water quality. The reverberations of his precedent-shattering action rippled through the whole structure of American government and industry. It signaled a fundamentally new approach to pollution control by Uncle Sam, one of toughness. Hickel had punctured all the assumptions that efforts to curb pollution could be safely put off until a later day.

It took over a year for the law suit to be settled. In the interim Secretary Hickel was fired and had returned to Alaska, and the federal water pollution program was transferred to the new Environmental Protection Agency. In August 1971, the company and the government began negotiations on the means to control the hot water. As head of EPA's enforcement program, I found myself in the middle of these negotiations, trying to find a solution to a problem that often seemed insoluble. Finally a consent decree was worked out, and I mailed a copy to Hickel up in Anchorage. The decree permitted the company to complete its nuclear units if it constructed a system to recycle the cooling water. The elaborate system consisted of a grid of thirty-eight canals, each about 5 miles long, 200 feet wide, and 4 feet deep. Water would be moved slowly through the canals until its heat was dissipated, and could then be recycled to the power plant and used again for cooling. The plan itself was controversial. Its cost was $35 million, and the system would cover seven thousand acres of land. Its completion, however, would eliminate the threat to the ecology of Biscayne Bay.

As I looked out from my perch in our helicopter at the expanse of everglades being transformed into the huge reservoir system, I marveled that a decision, made a year or two earlier, by one man sitting alone in the back seat of his car in Washington could cause dredges and bulldozers literally to change the face of the earth a thousand miles away. Already Hickel's decision to sue Florida Power and Light was receding into history, its outline mingling with dozens of subsequent actions. Yet at the time, Hickel's decision had been fateful, dramatic, and jolting.

The suit against Florida Power and Light was only one of Hickel's battles to protect the environment. Three months later, when it was discovered that some industrial plants were discharging mercury, and threatening public health, he responded at once by suing ten of the companies, and obtained immediate controls. Hickel broke other precedents by stepping into a local controversy in Beaufort, South Carolina; he blocked construction of a big BASF petrochemical plant in an area of valuable fisheries and natural beauty. His first strong actions had come in response to the Santa Barbara oil spill. Subsequently, when a big spill occurred off Louisiana at a Chevron platform not equipped with the required storm choke, Hickel demanded the company be prosecuted, and Chevron paid a fine of $1 million. He also banned a long list of persistent pesticides from use on any lands managed by the Department of the Interior.

These actions were among the decisive ones of that transition period in 1969 and 1970 when America began to adopt new attitudes toward her environment. Each event advanced the forces of change. But what about the man who made the decisions? To Wally Hickel these issues presented a personal challenge, filled with hard questions and political risks. That is how government policy takes shape. When one man must examine both his own convictions and conflicting public demands in order to make a decision, he will be subject to the broad forces of social change that produce the drama of human events. Again I asked myself what had made Wally Hickel take those audacious steps.

I had puzzled over the question before, and it continued to intrigue me. During the year I worked for Hickel I came to know him quite well. I knew how he talked and I knew how he thought. I liked him and admired him, but was never sure that I knew what made him tick. Part of the Hickel record reflected the combative spirit of the man. Another might have shrunk from making the tough decisions. But there was more. Much more. When Hickel became Secretary of the Interior, the clamor for environmental protection was being heard throughout the country. Old assumptions that set the patterns of government action were breaking under public pressure. Had the man made the events or had events made the man? Hickel's case was a mystery. It involved events that had taken place before I came to work at the Department of the Interior. While the huge rotor of the helicopter roared overhead, my mind ran back even further, to all I had heard of the Hickel confirmation hearings.

When Hickel was picked by President-elect Nixon in late 1968 to be Secretary of the Interior, he had no national reputation, but his qualifications seemed solid. He was an attractive, articulate, self-made man and Governor of Alaska. Wally Hickel had grown up in rural Kansas, lived through the Depression years as a teenager on a tenant farm, won a boxing championship in the Golden Gloves, and at the age of twenty left home to seek his fortune. He wound up in

Anchorage, Alaska, with thirty-seven cents in his pocket, and there he stayed, achieving success first in business and then in politics. It was a record that had appealed to the newly elected President, who admired self-made men, especially if they had made a lot of money. But Hickel's record was exposed to attack from an unexpected quarter.

Through his past activities Hickel had become identified with the interests of business, especially Big Oil. He confirmed that identification by some ill-considered comments he made after being picked by Nixon. Climbing off an airplane in Seattle at three-thirty one morning, he suggested that he might reverse a decision by Secretary Stewart Udall that froze development of 250 million acres of Alaska. He was quoted as questioning a policy of "conservation for conservation's sake," and he indicated that it didn't make sense to withdraw large areas of wilderness for conservation purposes and "lock it up for no reason." Then, too, he had allowed himself to be guided through a series of courtesy calls on Senators by an aide from the U.S. Chamber of Commerce. The publicity given these happenings and the public reaction to them were staggering.

The Senate Interior Committee, which was to review his nomination, received volumes of protest mail. In response to this outpouring of hostile comment, the committee set Hickel down for a grilling. Television floodlights and swarms of spectators jammed into the large hearing room, and one Senator after another cross-examined Hickel on his attitudes toward every phase of the operations of the Interior Department. They also queried him on the details of his personal business operations and the decisions he had made as Governor of Alaska. While other nominees for Cabinet posts were sailing through their confirmation hearings in a few hours of easy questions, Hickel's ordeal lasted, morning and afternoon, for four full days. He was on the defensive and under sharp attack. A Herblock cartoon told the story; it pictured Nixon leading his new Cabinet team in a triumphal march,

with Hickel stumbling along several steps behind and struggling to pull up his trousers. Those hearings left their mark
indelibly on the mind and memory of Wally Hickel.

It was later to become a popular myth that Hickel had
been converted into an environmentalist by the criticism he
received in his confirmation hearings. The conclusion seems
unfair. Beneath his eager assertiveness Hickel was a sensitive
man, and the hearings had certainly had an impact on his
thinking. He referred to them on occasion, always jokingly,
but with a poignancy that made clear that they had not been
a joke at the time. Yet Hickel was also open-minded and had
a vision for the future. He did not need to endure the trial of
the hearings to be made aware of the new concern about the
environment.

In 1969 the signs of that concern were everywhere. They
were manifest in the outcry against the Santa Barbara oil
spill, which occurred just one week after Hickel was
confirmed. They were seen in protests against projects as
distant and diverse as a Miami jetport, which threatened the
Everglades National Park in Florida, or the oil pipeline,
which threatened the tundra in Alaska. In cities across the
country, citizen environmentalists campaigned, with rising
success, against new highways that would destroy urban
parks or recreation areas. People were demanding a change
in the old policy toward the nation's resources.

The origins of the new concern were manifold: Los Angeles smog, Rachel Carson's *Silent Spring,* closures of beaches and shellfish beds, foaming detergents, the Cuyahoga
River's catching fire. All these indicated uncontrolled environmental decay. And when the astronauts in their space-
ship came back from the moon, their photographs showed
clouds of pollution hovering over North America. For years
the environment had remained the interest of only an active
few. In the late 1960s it suddenly caught hold. A sense of
alarm swept across the country. The press and television
discovered a "story" worth covering. Everywhere one

turned, another example of abuse appeared, to shock and dismay.

Political leaders began to respond. When the League of Women Voters and a combination of environmental organizations mounted a Crusade for Clean Water, Congress quadrupled its appropriations for building municipal sewage treatment plants. In the White House, Richard Nixon reportedly studied a poll showing that protection of the environment had become the third most important issue to the voters, and directed an aide to prepare a program that would put him on the right side of the issue. Toward the end of 1969, Congress enacted the National Environmental Policy Act, whose Section 102(2)(c) laid down requirements for writing environmental impact statements. But the most vivid demonstration of the power of the new environmental movement was yet to come.

It was Earth Day, April 22, 1970.

The event seemed to be spontaneous. It was sponsored by Senator Gaylord Nelson of Wisconsin and promoted by a small group of volunteers in their twenties. But suddenly it gathered momentum. Rallies of up to twenty-five thousand people were held in New York, Philadelphia, Chicago, and other cities. Fifth Avenue in New York was closed to automobiles, and traffic was rerouted in many other cities. In Washington an estimated ten thousand persons crowded the grounds of the Washington Monument. "Teach-ins" were held at schools and universities. Cleanup efforts were widespread. Gangs of local volunteers waded into stinking rivers and pulled junk and debris out of the water or picked up truckloads of litter from city streets.

The effect of Earth Day could not be missed. It made front-page news in every newspaper; stirred excitement in every city. It was celebrated at some two thousand university campuses and at roughly ten thousand grammar and high schools. Estimates were that ten million public school children participated in the teach-ins. The spontaneity, size, and intensity evident in the thousands of demonstrations across the land left no doubt that Americans were gripped by the new concern. Earth Day had been, as *Time* magazine put it, the nation's "biggest street festival since the Japanese surrender in 1945."

It was in this context of public protest and political response that Wally Hickel became an environmental leader. He felt the force of citizen action, and he felt it directly. It came at him from every source: in the mail, in the press, on TV, through personal conversations, and certainly in the response by citizens to the decisions he made. When Hickel's intervention blocked the petrochemical plant in Beaufort, a shrimp boat sailed to Washington and personally delivered two large cardboard boxes containing the signatures of forty-five thousand local residents expressing their thanks.

Hickel was not a giant in the environmental movement. Many others have had a deeper and more lasting impact. But for the nearly two years he served as Interior Secretary, Wally Hickel became something of a symbol of the new approach to environmental issues. He deserves that credit. He had courage. He stood where the opposing pressures collided, and he made difficult decisions to preserve and protect. The irony is that Hickel was never cut out to be an environmental leader. He was a businessman and developer first, a political leader second, and an environmentalist only when the occasion arose. Yet in a curious way this makes his role as a symbol even more appropriate. In our democratic political system, leaders do not simply appear at the moment of their choice. Instead, they emerge when deeper forces determine the need for them. The real power behind Wally Hickel's bold actions was the eruption of citizen protest, the demand that government do something to save the environment.

And as I looked from the helicopter at a dragline dredging the swamp beneath me, I knew that the power of that protest could, in fact, change the face of this earth.

CHAPTER 2

The Birth of EPA

RICHARD NIXON never became a hero of the environmentalists. Yet the record of the Nixon Administration included
strong support for many environmental programs. The President's Environmental Messages, submitted to Congress in
1970 and 1971, gave impetus to the enactment of far-
reaching environmental statutes. In addition, the Nixon Administration was solely responsible for one of the major
achievements of the environmental movement: the creation
of the Environmental Protection Agency.

The origins of the new agency date back to January 1970,
when a blue-ribbon presidential council on government
reorganization (known as the Ash Council, after its chairman,
Roy Ash) began to examine the programs dealing with
natural resources. That was part of a broad effort to stream-
line government operations, a goal that President Nixon had
personally emphasized. After weeks of quiet study, the
council's staff prepared an ambitious proposal, recommend-
ing the creation of a huge new department. One morning the
staff members came over to Interior to explain their plan to
Secretary Hickel. To the left of the Secretary's desk they set
up on a tripod a large chart graphically outlining the
proposal. An elaborate diagram of lines and boxes set forth
their grand design to reshuffle bureaus, offices, and divisions
from a variety of departments and agencies into a new
colossus: the "Department of Natural Resources and the
Environment."

As a staff aide, I sat on the sofa along the wall to Hickel's right and listened intently to the presentation. I looked at the chart with a sense of bewilderment, and studied all the boxes, trying to comprehend the programs and people they represented. The proposed department would be mammoth, like another Department of Defense; it would combine nearly all of the federal programs concerning pollution control, public lands, natural resources, and energy. It was to be built around the Department of Interior, but would be greatly expanded by the addition of important programs from the Departments of Agriculture; Health, Education, and Welfare; and Commerce; and from the Corps of Engineers; the Atomic Energy Commission; and other federal agencies.

This ambitious proposal triggered an immediate conflict in the Cabinet over who would control which parts of government turf. Secretary Hickel stood to be the big winner, but some other Cabinet officers would be losers, especially Secretary Clifford Hardin, whose Department of Agriculture stood to lose the Forest Service and much of the Soil Conservation Service. Maurice Stans, Secretary of Commerce, faced the prospect of having the U.S. Weather Bureau and several other programs taken from his department, which was small to begin with.

Two principal weapons were to be used in the fray. One was the personal clout of the Cabinet officers who would be affected. The other was the "merits" of the staff proposal. The power of each was difficult to assess, and the stakes were high. The outcome of the contest could determine the course of government programs for years, even decades. Secretary Hickel entered the lists with gusto, and when his turn came, he stated the issue with his usual down-to-earth eloquence. He argued that "you cannot separate the environment from natural resources" and that all the related programs had to be placed in a single department. Riding back from the White House after delivering his argument, Wally Hickel turned to me in the back seat of his limousine, both his face and his voice sparkling with enthusiasm, and declared, "I want to be the last Secretary of the Interior and the first Secretary of the Department of Natural Resources and the Environment!"

We could only speculate on the thoughts of the members of the President's council. Many factors had to be weighed, including personalities. Looking at the array of programs covered by the proposed new department, insiders wondered, will the President be willing to hand all that to Wally Hickel? The truth is that no government decision, however big, is made in a vacuum. It is always a piece of a larger puzzle, subject to influence by unrelated factors. In this instance, the proposal to create a vastly expanded department built around Interior was to be influenced by the fact that the Secretary of the Interior was Wally Hickel, a man who had never been on solid terms with President Nixon. His management of the Interior Department had long been criticized by the White House staff. Moreover, the relationship between Hickel and Nixon was about to be jolted by an event that had nothing to do with natural resources and the environment. In the first week of May 1970, Hickel went off like a skyrocket.

At Kent State University in Ohio, National Guardsmen had just killed four students who were protesting the American invasion of Cambodia. Students across the country cried out in protest. A weekly staff meeting was held in the large, wood-paneled Secretary's conference room on the fifth floor of the Interior building the following Tuesday morning, and it was obvious to all of us that Hickel was deeply upset. He swept aside the agenda of regular business and led a long, rambling, emotional discussion, principally with two members of his personal staff who were themselves just over college age. What angered them most was the White House response to the killings, which was a terse, unsympathetic release stating that when dissent turns to violence it leads to tragedy. It seemed to be pointing the finger of blame at the dead students. Hickel left the meeting, rode the tiny, special elevator back up to his own office on the sixth floor, and canceled all appointments for the day. Like others in the department, I had no idea what was about to happen, but the biggest public drama in Wally Hickel's life was quietly beginning.

The next day, just before noon, I was in a meeting in Hickel's office. In the midst of the discussion, the telephone suddenly rang. Since ordinary calls were received in the outer office, the ringing of the phone startled us, and Hickel reacted as though he had heard an alarm. His right arm shot up in an abrupt gesture to quiet our talk. "Hold it, fellas! This could be important," he called out as his left hand reached out to the oversized white telephone on his desk. "Why? What? It couldn't have!" he said with force into the phone, his face flushing with color. But it had, and Wally Hickel's life in Washington would never again be the same. The rest of us in the room had no idea what had happened, but none could miss the tension on Hickel's face and in his voice. In silence we exchanged glances, while my mind raced wildly wondering what had been said at the other end of the line.

The caller was President Nixon's top aide, H. R. Haldeman, calling from the White House, and he had been blazing mad. Quickly the story began to unfold. All during the previous day, Hickel had been distraught over the Cambodian invasion, the Kent State killings, and the attitudes of the White House toward young people protesting against the Vietnam War. After trying fruitlessly to reach the President, Hickel wrote him a letter that was strongly worded, deeply felt, and sharply critical. It stated that our own history clearly shows "that youth in its protest must be heard." Hickel had polished the letter that morning and sent it over to the White House an hour or so before. Within a half hour or forty-five

minutes it was on the AP wire, flashing into newsrooms across
the country. When Haldeman called he had the letter — and
the wire story too.

The letter created a national sensation and caused a
wave of rumor and speculation within the department. It was
obvious from the timing that the leak had come from
Interior, and within Hickel's staff suspicions were strong
that he had directed it himself. One rumor was that he
had second thoughts and had attempted to retrieve the
letter from Roberta Hornig of the Washington *Star,* but
that she had refused to cooperate because the AP was
already running the story. People gossiped about motives and
about the probable consequences. "He's a marked man now.
You wait and see," my secretary, Lee Tucker, said know-
ingly. "The White House will never let him get away with
this."

Anticipation that Hickel might be promptly fired,
however, was offset by the reaction of the national press.
Hickel had become an instant hero. His letter was translated
into dozens of languages and reprinted all over the world. In
the media blitz that followed, Hickel was totally swept away
from the routine work of the department. He was a new and
popular celebrity, and while observers speculated how long
he would stay in his post, Wally Hickel used its power for all
he was worth. At the end of the first week he received a clear
warning signal about the future: he was abruptly "disinvited"
from worship services at the White House the following
Sunday. Yet he was to remain in the Cabinet for another six
months, until after the 1970 elections.

How Hickel's letter affected the deliberations on reorganization, just then coming to a head, is a matter of pure
conjecture. Certainly his timing could not have been worse.
His letter offended the President just when the President's
staff was considering the proposal that would have elevated
Hickel. One cannot help speculating that if the Secretary of

the Interior had had a close relationship with the President, the proposal to assign the environmental programs to the Interior Department might have been adopted, and the subsequent history of the environmental movement certainly would have been different from what it has been.

We received no immediate response after Secretary Hickel and the other Cabinet officers made their arguments before the Ash Council. It was known that as a result of the furor Hickel had considered resigning as Interior Secretary to return to Alaska and run for election to the Senate or for another term as Governor. Under Alaska law he faced a filing deadline, the first of June, to declare his intention to be a candidate. That day came and passed. At 8:20 the very next morning Hickel received a call, spelling out the decision on reorganization. The pollution control programs would be established as a separate agency (EPA), and a second narrow group of programs would be reorganized into a National Oceanic and Atmospheric Administration within the Department of Commerce. All the rest of the proposal to create a Department of Natural Resources and the Environment was to be shelved.

In personal terms the decision was a victory for Maurice Stans, long a loyal supporter of President Nixon's, whose Department of Commerce not only lost no authority, but indeed acquired a cluster of new ones. It was also a victory for Clifford Hardin, whose Department of Agriculture remained nearly intact. And it was a defeat for Wally Hickel. He lost his chance to head the proposed gigantic department, and saw Interior lose a couple of its major programs, including the water pollution control program, in which he had taken a great personal interest. It was typical of Hickel's recklessness that while this major decision was pending he had tilted with the White House.

The decision must also be viewed from other angles. In political terms it was a compromise that reduced opposition to the reorganization. The original proposal might well have been too bold, since vested interests would have tried to lobby for its overturn in the Congress. One irony that is intriguing to ponder is that by adopting the more modest proposal the President inadvertently may have established a more powerful agency to fight for environmental reform. When one considers the vigor and independence that have characterized EPA, one can readily believe that the federal pollution control programs would not have been as effective as they are had they been buried in the huge bureaucracy the new department would have created.

Even more interesting than speculation over the choice of the reorganization plan, however, is the fact that President Nixon did make a major change in the government in order to strengthen its effectiveness in tackling environmental problems. It is hard to believe that he did so out of personal concern for environmental protection. There is little to suggest that President Nixon had any strong interest in that area, and certainly after EPA was formed he gave it little time or attention. Instead, the explanation is to be found in deeper forces running through the country. The rising public concern over pollution created pressure for government action. That pressure called attention to the fact that the government was poorly organized to address these problems. The Nixon reorganization experts were neither proponents nor opponents of environmental reform; their specialty was management and organization. The reason they focused on the environment must have been because that was the area in which political pressures were creating a demand for action. The creation of EPA thus suggests the power of the American presidency to respond to the needs of the public quite apart from the goals and aspirations of the man who is the President.

On July 2, 1970, President Nixon sent to Congress reorganization plans to create the Environmental Protection Agency and the National Oceanic and Atmospheric Administration. Under the Reorganization Act of 1948, the two proposals became effective sixty days later, since neither the House nor the Senate took adverse action against them. This meant that EPA would come into existence under law and commence operations on December 2, 1970. The attention of everyone working on preparations to establish the new Environmental Protection Agency immediately shifted to the next major question — the selection of the first Administrator.

We all hoped the President would make an early appointment. The sooner the new leader was named, the more time he would have to begin filling other top positions so that the whole agency could start off strong. In addition, 1970 was an election year, and there would probably be a bumper crop of defeated candidates looking for jobs on the morning of November 3. Our fear was that the job of EPA Administrator would go as a consolation prize to one of the party faithful who might have little administrative competence and no environmental commitment. As September and October rolled by with no White House announcement, it became apparent that the appointment would not be made until after the election.

What we had no inkling of at the time was the actions, taking place behind the scenes, that were to determine the choice. They had begun several months before. In the summer of 1970, even after the President's reorganization proposals were announced, few people were aware of the plans to create a new environmental agency. One of those who were aware was Gerald Hansler, a career officer in the U.S. Public Health Service, stationed in New York to oversee implementation of the federal air pollution controls. Jerry Hansler, however, was not just another career civil servant. In addition to his professional training, he also had an unusual mixture of imagination, enthusiasm, and political skill (some of which he may have picked up from his father-in-law, the U.S. Senator from North Carolina, Sam Ervin).

When Jerry Hansler heard of the President's reorganization proposals, his fertile imagination went to work. Acting entirely on his own initiative, he picked up the telephone one day and placed a long-distance call to an old friend, Bill Ruckelshaus. "How would you like to be the head of EPA?" he asked. The reply was another question. "What's EPA?" Hansler explained that a new agency was going to be formed to take over federal programs to control pollution, and there was a question about who its director would be.

Hansler had met Ruckelshaus in the early 1960s, when he was assigned to the Indiana State Health Department and Ruckelshaus was working for the State of Indiana as an Assistant Attorney General. Ruckelshaus became Hansler's lawyer and Hansler was Ruckelshaus's star witness, and together they brought suit against polluters in a state with plenty of pollution. "Jerry had a white plastic fish he would put in the water and photograph to show how bad the pollution was. It wasn't till the third trial that I learned the fish was plastic," Bill later recalled. In those days the methods of proof were a bit crude, but the pollution was overpowering and judges liked the pictures. Jerry Hansler was a practical man and always a fighter, and he found in Ruckelshaus an effective ally. Years later when he caught wind of the proposed new EPA he remembered his old compatriot from the Indiana days and wondered if he wouldn't be good for the top job in the new agency.

When Jerry Hansler finished his explanation, Ruckelshaus was noncommittal. Hansler was undeterred. Would Bill mind "if I surfaced your name?" "Surfaced with who?" Bill asked. Hansler rattled off a list of national leaders in pollution control. Ruckelshaus had never heard of any of them, but said he would not object. They both hung up. Ruckelshaus's curiosity was piqued. Hansler's interest was encouraged. He began to plan his next moves.

Bill Ruckelshaus's record did not give Jerry Hansler a lot to work with. Except for his stint in the Indiana AG's office, Bill had virtually no background in environmental problems. He had grown up in Indiana and gone off for his education to Princeton and Harvard Law School. Returning home, he practiced law for a short while, then served in the state government, and rose rapidly in the state Republican Party. In 1968 he ran for the U.S. Senate but was soundly beaten by the incumbent, Birch Bayh. After that he had moved to Washington where he became a United States Assistant Attorney General. Hansler took that record and infused it with his own enthusiasm. He began a quiet campaign to sell Ruckelshaus to leaders of environmental organizations, professional groups, and others concerned with control of pollution. Step by step he built up a list of prominent figures willing to sign up in support of Bill Ruckelshaus.

The endorsements gathered by Hansler assured that Ruckelshaus at least would be considered as a candidate for head of EPA. What gave his candidacy the extra needed push was support from another quarter. During his two years in Washington, Ruckelshaus had earned the respect and friendship of his boss, Attorney General John Mitchell, and the power of John Mitchell in the Nixon Administration was unsurpassed. Mitchell one day was riding in his limousine across the Fourteenth Street Bridge over the Potomac to Virginia. The question of appointing someone to run the new EPA cropped up in the conversation, and Mitchell casually remarked that Bill Ruckelshaus did not really want the job. Mitchell's press aide took note of the comment, which he thought was a complete misunderstanding, and relayed it to Ruckelshaus. Astonished to learn of Mitchell's impression, Ruckelshaus went straight to him and explained that he definitely hoped to be appointed. Once that was done, the rest was easy. Mitchell promptly telephoned the President and threw his weight behind Ruckelshaus. It is another of the ironies of the Washington scene that John Mitchell, who later became one of the villains of Watergate, played a decisive role in the appointment of Ruckelshaus to the job in which he was to become "Mr. Clean."

At the time, I knew nothing of all these maneuverings. In mid-November I made a trip to Florida to talk with Interior Department officials working under the agreement that had blocked the new Miami jetport, which threatened the ecology of the Everglades National Park. It was on that trip that I first heard of the appointment. Our car was cruising along the causeway from Virginia Key across to Miami. It was a fall day, filled with sunshine, and the pressures and bustle of Washington seemed a world away. Suddenly my ears pricked up to the newscast coming from the radio: "The White House announced today that President Nixon will nominate as the first Administrator of the Environmental Protection Agency William Ruckels . . ." William who? I had never heard the name of the man who was soon to become my new leader.

I returned to Washinngton on Sunday night. On Monday morning the first item on my schedule was a meeting at the Council on Environmental Quality to review a proposal that the President establish a permit program covering water pollution from industrial plants. There, to my surprise, I met Bill Ruckelshaus, and in the discussion at that lengthy session we became acquainted with each other. It was a chance meeting, something that easily might not have occurred. But that first meeting was to lead to further contacts and result in my staying in Washington and becoming engaged in the environmental battle for many years longer than I had ever dreamed or intended.

Shortly afterward I was contacted by a person working for Ruckelshaus. To my amazement he asked if I would be interested in taking one of the principal jobs at EPA. Though the details were still vague, he was able to tell me that it would involve being both the agency's first General Counsel and its Assistant Administrator in charge of the enforcement program. The prospect filled me with excitement; I was thirty-five and ready to accept the challenge. I rushed together a résumé, and a few days later an interview with Bill Ruckelshaus was arranged.

I met with Ruckelshaus in the office that had been found for him on a short-term lease. It was an impressively big room, but it looked as if the movers had just brought in the furniture. Things were strewn about in random fashion, and on one side of the room a collection of file folders and cartons lay in a heap on the floor. Despite that setting and the vast responsibilities that were about to land on him, Ruckelshaus seemed entirely relaxed. We sat down in a couple of chairs in one corner of the room, and he came directly to the point. He said that he had talked to several people about me and wanted me to take the job. He did not even go through the pretense of conducting an interview; he made a firm offer, and I accepted eagerly.

I learned later that that was typical of the Ruckelshaus manner — he never wasted time on formalities or beating around the bush. In a matter of two or three minutes we had established a cooperative and working relationship. Bill casually changed subjects, and we spent the rest of the thirty minutes discussing a pending decision. Our meeting opened the door to a world that was wholly new to me, but it had happened so quickly and calmly that when I left his office I could hardly believe that world was real. The directness and informality were characteristic of the earliest days at EPA. Ruckelshaus was hiring key officials and making important decisions that would affect EPA for years to come, but he was doing it in a manner that was close to nonchalance.

It turned out that the timing of my shift to EPA seemed to bear the approval of providence. Within a week or ten days all the details were worked out, and on the Tuesday before Thanksgiving I informed Secretary Hickel that I had accepted the job at EPA. The following afternoon, while I was driving home from work, the final act in Hickel's drama with the White House was played out. Hickel, who had been called on short notice to a meeting in the White House, was ushered in to see President Nixon and brusquely informed that he was fired. Minutes later I heard the news over my car radio. Nor was that all. That Friday Fred Malek came over to Interior from the White House and in curt, ten-minute meetings fired several members of Hickel's top staff, men I had worked with throughout the previous year. He directed them to clean out their desks immediately and be out of the building for good by the end of the day. On Monday morning when I entered the building their names had already been removed from the directory on the wall. Among the names listed in the Office of the Secretary mine was the only one left. I assumed that I had been passed over partly because I was moving to EPA. With a sense of having had a narrow escape, I knew how glad I was to have the new job.

Since all work in the Office of the Secretary of the Interior ground to an immediate halt, I was free at once to concentrate on the activities at EPA. There my first interest was to learn more about my new boss, the man who had come out of nowhere to take charge of the new agency. My first chance to watch him in action was at his confirmation hearings.

The special session of the Public Works Committee had been shifted from the committee's usual hearing room on the fourth floor of the New Senate Office Building to a slightly larger room on the first floor. Even so, when I arrived there was standing room only, with people jammed into every bit of available space. I squeezed in near the back of the crowd and looked around the room. Under the lights, a battery of television cameras stood waiting. The panel seats for the members of the committee, so often more than half vacant, were all filled. I knew that Bill had been extensively briefed by officials from many different programs to be fused into EPA, but I wondered nervously how well he would do. I thought about Wally Hickel and how quickly the merry-go-round revolves in Washington. Just eight months before, Hickel had expected that all these programs would be put in Interior with himself in charge. Now a new agency had been established, with a new face to head it, and Hickel was back in Alaska. I recalled Hickel's confirmation hearings and the grilling he had been given, and I wondered if Ruckelshaus would have to endure similar fire.

As the morning progressed, the questioning by Senator after Senator, though not unfriendly, was thorough, and fully tested all of Bill's training and homework. Before an audience straining for a first insight into this man who would hold so much authority, Ruckelshaus gave an almost perfect performance. He was relaxed and articulate in answering questions, flashing an occasional twinkle of humor. He stated his determination to take any action required to achieve environmental protection, and displayed a surprising familiarity with the programs he was about to inherit, though he was candid in admitting his lack of knowledge about various subjects that were raised. The hearings lasted two days, and were fully attended. At the beginning there were no significant doubts as to his confirmation, and at the end there was none at all. Ruckelshaus had obviously made a favorable impression. "What that does," said Doug Costle, who had been on the Ash Council staff, "is to buy you time to get organized before the criticism sets in." Bill's confirmation came on December 3, one day after the Environmental Protection Agency officially commenced operations.

The confirmation hearings had revealed publicly one of the chief capabilities of Bill Ruckelshaus — his skill under the lights and before the microphones. He had a natural talent for public appearance, an ability to be open and articulate in expressing himself and to convey a sense of honesty and purpose. To those who had watched him bone up for the session, the hearings revealed another attribute — his willingness to work tirelessly to prepare for such an appearance. There was still another feature of Bill's make-up that I was about to discover — his readiness to make decisions quickly when faced with complex problems. Amid the frenzy of the first few weeks at EPA, a crisis was to arise that would test this strength. It involved a proposed substitute, NTA, for phosphates in detergents.

One of the most critical and widely publicized problems in water pollution had been eutrophication of lakes. Eutrophication, a natural process in the aging of lakes, is the concentration of nutrients which are increased by run-off from surrounding land and reduce the oxygen content of the water. Under the impact of man's activities, this process, which normally would occur over a long span of geologic time, has been abruptly telescoped. Two of the chief causes of this speed-up were the heavy use of commerical fertilizers and the presence of phosphates in detergents. As a result of eutrophication, lake waters lose their crystal-clear quality and become murky through the growth of algae. In extreme cases heavy "blooms" of algae growth occur, and as they decompose they release a putrid odor. In an attempt to halt acceleration of eutrophication, the government had been pushing detergent manufacturers to reduce or eliminate phosphates in detergents and to use in their stead a substitute developed through private research, nitrilotriacetic acid, or NTA.

In response to government pressure, chemical companies had invested over $100 million in facilities to produce NTA, and the leading detergent makers were beginning to use it. Nothing was known at the outset about the effects, if any, of NTA, on the environment or health, but research was undertaken. In November a research project conducted by the Food and Drug Administration was completed. It suggested that the presence of NTA in a water supply might lead to birth defects and other dangers to health. Dave Stephan, a top member of the water pollution research program that was now part of EPA, reviewed the FDA research report. A week after EPA was formed, he sent a memo to Ruckelshaus stating that in his judgment NTA presented serious risks to health and urging that the government require the detergent companies immediately to cease all use of NTA.

For Ruckelshaus, it was a hot potato, and he had almost no one to turn to for support. The health warning was serious, but since the research results were preliminary they might not stand up under further testing. The tough question, therefore, was whether immediate abandonment of NTA should be demanded prior to further research. It would be embarrassing for the government to demand that industry stop using NTA, because just a year before the government had demanded that industry start using it. In addition, rejection of NTA would wreck the whole program to remove phosphates from detergents and undercut the entire effort against lake eutrophication.

Ruckelshaus did not know Dave Stephan and could not know how reliable his judgment was. One risk was clear, however—the Stephan memo might soon leak to the press. It could be a disaster for EPA if it appeared that Ruckelshaus was sitting on a recommendation that he take emergency action. "I'd love to be Dave Stephan," said Bill's press aide, Bob Teeter. "He's in a perfect position." Ruckelshaus laughed, but he also knew that he was on the horns of a dilemma, and he was squirming. Still, he had no choice but to face the crisis head-on, to dig into the facts and make the best decision he could without delay. During the first two weeks of his term as Administrator, Ruckelshaus thus found himself spending whole mornings and afternoons examining the

research results on NTA and considering what action should
be taken. After a few days' consideration, Ruckelshaus and
top officials at the Department of Health, Education, and
Welfare agreed that use of NTA should be stopped.

The procedures followed to implement that decision took
me by surprise. No law provided legal authority to require
the industry to drop NTA. Instead, the leading companies in
the industry were abruptly summoned to send representatives to a meeting to be held the very next day. The plan was
simply to give them the bad news and call for "voluntary"
action to abandon NTA.

Before the meeting, the government officials met in the
office of Jesse Steinfeld, the Surgeon General, for a strategy
session. Proposals for how we should handle the meeting
bobbled back and forth. Finally, Billy Goodrich, the top
lawyer for FDA, broke in on the tangled discussion. "I've
been through quite a number of these," he said with a smile
of authority that brought quiet to the room. "So let me tell
you how it's going to go." He explained that we would have
to start off by explaining our research results and what we
proposed. Then we should sit back and wait for the industry
to counterattack. The response of its spokesmen would come
in two waves. First they would complain bitterly over the
government's change of position and beat that around for all
it was worth. Then they would go after the research tests and
challenge their reliability. "At this point," Goodrich said,
looking up with a chuckle at the group of us around him
hanging on every word, "it all depends on my friend Bill,"
pointing to Ruckelshaus with one hand, "and my friend
Jesse," pointing to Steinfeld with the other. "If they blink —
even once — the game is over." Billy Goodrich was a short,
jovial, knowing sort of man, and it didn't take long for us
amateurs to figure out that he was a pro. We paid attention
and took his instructions. Then we filed out of Steinfeld's
office and headed down to the conference room, where two
dozen industry representatives were seated around a long

conference table, waiting for a surprise they knew they weren't going to like.

Ruckelshaus, Steinfeld, and Goodrich took seats at one end of the long table, surrounded by a few other government people. I found a seat partway down one side and sat down next to Jim Lynn, General Counsel of the Department of Commerce, who was muttering that the whole scene was incredible and disastrous. With intense curiosity (and a variety of other feelings) I waited for the action to begin. The meeting proceeded exactly as Billy Goodrich had predicted. First the government presented its position: NTA had been found to have adverse health effects and the government wished to obtain a voluntary agreement from industry not to use it any more; the government hoped to make an announcement, at a press conference scheduled for that afternoon, praising industry for its cooperation; but if industry did not agree, government officials would feel compelled to hold a press conference anyway and announce the results of their research.

I looked up and down the table at the businessmen seated around me, their faces expressing, alternately, astonishment, anger, resentment, and resignation. Again, just as Billy Goodrich had predicted, they challenged first the abrupt procedure and then the research results. As I listened to the heated arguments, I wondered how reliable the research was. I remembered the cranberry scare of the 1950s, when the government claims had been wrong. Yet it was clear in this instance that the research results would rule the day. The industry representatives protested bitterly, but they knew where power lay. It was government by press release, but there was no recourse. Ruckelshaus and Steinfeld had not blinked. The government announcement would force the abandonment of NTA no matter what they did, and with not much more than a whimper they consented to go along with the proposal.

At a press conference held in the afternoon of December

18, 1970, U.S. Surgeon General Jesse Steinfeld and EPA Administrator William Ruckelshaus announced that research results had indicated that NTA posed health risks, and they praised industry for agreeing to abandon use of NTA. In the course of the matter Ruckelshaus had picked up a quick education. Ten days before he had never heard of nitrilotriacetic acid, but, standing on the platform, he was able to describe authoritatively the scientific evidence and the rationale for the government action. I watched his performance with growing respect. He looked for all the world as if he knew what he was talking about.

NTA was one instance of a crisis exploding in our path. There were many others, individually less dramatic but in their total imposing a tremendous burden. They involved work on the budget for the coming year, an ambitious legislative program to be presented to Congress, new enforcement actions, a flood of requests for interviews and speeches, and countless others, all pressing for action. Many had impossible deadlines. Of necessity, staffing and organizational problems were handled on the fly. It was, as Ruckelshaus often quipped, like running the 100-yard dash and taking your own appendix out at the same time.

Of all these urgent matters the most important was the selection by Ruckelshaus of people to make up his top management, and Bill quickly revealed a sense of independence in his selections. He picked Democrats to fill a number of major positions. Before long, flak began to come from the direction of the White House. At first this did not bother Ruckelshaus, though after a while he did feel constrained to give the White House more weight when making his choices. If an agency is to have the support of the Chief Executive, its personnel selection must not cause a lot of friction. At one point I commented, "Bill, you and I come from the opposite ends of the earth in this regard. You've been at the Justice Department, where John Mitchell sits at the right hand of the President and his subordinates can do no wrong. I was at Interior, where Wally Hickel had no strength in the White House at all and we were constantly being sniped at by everyone in the White House and OMB [the Office of Management and Budget]. You have to strike a balance. If you get those fellows turned against you, the agency will suffer in ways we can't even foresee."

Bill Ruckelshaus's readiness to strike out on his own, however, soon turned to my advantage. Among the positions that I was filling was that of Legislative Counsel for the agency. One candidate I interviewed was a staff assistant to Senator Robert Dole of Kansas. Though I made it clear that I was interviewing many others for the job, I said frankly that I had no definite choice in mind. The young man assumed that, because of his strong political support, he would be given the job. When I called to say that I had made a different choice, he erupted.

In a bit of a panic I dashed down the two flights of stairs and explained the situation to Ruckelshaus. Before I finished, the Senator was on the telephone, blasting my decision. Though Senator Dole was then the Republican National Chairman, and as such, had a good deal of influence in the White House, Ruckelshaus appeared not the least bit concerned. He had no patience with the Senator's complaint and had no thought but to support my choice. "Dole's just trying to throw his weight around," he said with a smile as he hung up the phone, and I went back up to my office feeling greatly reassured. A month or so later, however, when the time came for me and three other Assistant Administrators to be confirmed, our confirmations were held up until Ruckelshaus made a special trip to visit with Dole and personally apologize for the disappointment we had caused his assistant. Even then Ruckelshaus was undeterred. He was willing to take the heat of political pressure but not to let it change his decision.

The self-confidence with which Bill Ruckelshaus made

hard decisions enabled him to be a strong leader when he had to address the unending series of problems that confronted EPA. Ruckelshaus knew that the country demanded action in attacking the environmental problems, and he did not agonize over the chance that a few mistakes might be made. This approach had a happy effect on those of us who worked for him. We felt his confidence in our judgment and knew that he would back us up if the going got rough. He was willing to delegate major responsibilities to his subordinates; this attitude was apparent in the way he organized the agency's regional offices.

The offices transferred into EPA at its start contained roughly six thousand employees, working in the fields of water pollution, air pollution, pesticides, solid wastes, and radiation. Except in the case of water pollution, none of the programs had a strong regional structure. The White House staff had recommended that EPA be made a showcase of decentralization, and Ruckelshaus took up the challenge. He decided that each regional organization should mirror the full EPA structure, with staff capabilities in every program area. He also resolved to delegate an extraordinary degree of responsibility to the regional offices, allowing them to run their operations without a constant stream of instructions from headquarters. As a result EPA became one of the most decentralized agencies in the federal government, an organizational structure that gave the agency a rare capability to make decisions, move programs ahead, and motivate people to produce high volumes of work. In view of the immense complexity of EPA's programs, the agency's progress would have been tightly restricted if it had not built a strong regional structure right from the start.

The early months of EPA sparkled with vitality, under Bill Ruckelshaus's leadership. We all were working exceedingly hard. For several months at the start I followed a schedule of rising every morning at five-thirty and driving in to reach the office before seven, often watching the sunrise light up the sky over the city as I drove along the George Washington Parkway. The workday would run until seven or eight in the evening, with almost no letup on the weekends. Although everyone was under intense pressure, the cheerful humor of Ruckelshaus soothed frictions and melted away fatigue. On weekends he would pad around the office in white tennis shoes and an old sweater or sweat shirt. In large meetings he would put his feet up on the table and laugh heartily at his own jokes or those of others. While we were in temporary quarters in the old Normandy Building, he would take over one of the antiquated elevators and operate it for a couple of runs, delivering people to their different floors. He was remarkably open, and staff members from all levels had easy access to him, which created bonds of loyalty throughout the agency. Ruckelshaus had a way of reaching people in a direct and unforced manner. He possessed that elusive talent to make people laugh, to make people work, and to make people believe in the possibility of a better day.

Outside the agency too, Ruckelshaus's reputation for achievement steadily grew. The excitement of the environmental movement created a sense of accomplishment that he seemed unconsciously to project. His clear statements and strong positions converted public enthusiasm into respect. Ruckelshaus had several advantages to build on in establishing his personal image as the attractive, effective Administrator of EPA. He had a new agency, an exciting issue, and a constituency that was grateful for the bold positions he was taking. And he capitalized on these advantages with skill. He quickly became a forceful spokesman for the public interest, creating a reservoir of support for the agency he headed.

While Ruckelshaus established his personal reputation and that of the EPA, he was also establishing the direction of EPA and building a framework of attitudes that would govern its course of action throughout the years ahead. The

long-term significance of the events of these early months
was far greater than any of us recognized at the time.

Ruckelshaus believed in the strength of public opinion and
public support. The organized environmental movement had
been formed because of public pressure, and Ruckelshaus
responded instinctively to that pressure. He did not seek
support for his actions in the established structures of
political power. He turned instead directly to the press and
to public opinion, often in conflict with those very structures.
In so doing he tied the fortunes of EPA to public opinion as
the only base of political support. The results were impressive, especially during the period of public clamor for
environmental reform, though that dependence created a
vulnerability; if ever the intensity of public support should
wane, so would the effectiveness of the agency.

Through the Ruckelshaus leadership basic policies developed within the EPA were shaped by the forces of public
opinion, just as the agency's creation was a consequence of
those same forces. The environmental movement demanded
strong action, and EPA responded to the pressures of the
grassroots political protest in all the decisions and actions
initiated by Bill Ruckelshaus as Administrator. The response
was reflected most clearly in his approach to enforcement.

CHAPTER 3

Prosecuting the Polluters

"THAT'S A politically motivated cheap shot!" Mayor Carl Stokes shouted into the microphone in a room crowded with mayors and reporters. Ruckelshaus was suddenly on the defensive as he confronted the furious Mayor of Cleveland following his announcements of enforcement actions against Cleveland, Atlanta, and Detroit. As I read the full account in the *New York Times* in the quiet of my office the next morning, I wished we had had more time for staff work before Bill made the announcement.

Ruckelshaus had been scheduled for a trip to Atlanta one week after his confirmation to address the annual convention of the National League of Cities. A gathering of several hundred mayors and other top city officials from all over the country would afford a national forum for him to make his first major policy speech. Ruckelshaus had been anxious to start momentum within EPA by immediately taking strong enforcement actions. He asked for staff recommendations for actions he could take quickly, and late one afternoon a few days before the Atlanta trip I drove over from the office I still had at Interior to EPA's temporary quarters at 20th and L streets to go over a group of proposals with him. Four or five of us sat in a circle with a heap of office file folders scattered about us on the floor. Each one contained a separate recommendation, and we went through them one by one, trying to figure out which to proceed with. One suggestion was that violation notices be issued to several large cities that had fallen behind their schedules to construct municipal sewage treatment plants. After a brief discussion, Ruckelshaus approved that idea and told me to prepare the notices against Atlanta, Cleveland, and Detroit.

We knew there would be full press coverage of the Atlanta speech and saw it as an advantage. Ruckelshaus would be face to face with the mayors. He could make a tough speech challenging the cities to meet their deadlines and threatening enforcement if they failed. The announcement that he was taking such action against three of the biggest cities in the country would dispel any doubts that Ruckelshaus would back up his threats with action.

The Atlanta speech did succeed in putting EPA's enforcement effort on the front pages, but not in the way we had hoped. As soon as Ruckelshaus made his announcement, Mayor Stokes of Cleveland, one of the country's first black mayors, jumped to his feet and mounted an emotional counterattack. He charged that the three cities had been picked because all had Democratic mayors. He also blamed the federal government for the very delays for which Ruckelshaus was criticizing the cities: the construction of the sewage treatment plants, he said, had been held back by a shortage of federal funds, the administration and Congress having failed to appropriate the money authorized in earlier statutes to finance the municipal construction program. Critics from Detroit and Atlanta repeated the charges.

The facts of the case seemed to support the accusations. It was true that federal funding for municipal construction grants had fallen far below the levels authorized in 1966, and a shortage of federal funds had indeed played a role in delaying completion of the facilities in Cleveland and Detroit. Even more embarrassing was the appearance that Ruckelshaus was not familiar with these facts at the time he announced the enforcement actions. The Atlanta speech did highlight Ruckelshaus's determination to get tough, but it raised a question as to how thorough his homework had been. From the White House came a warning by presidential aide John Whitaker: "If Ruck becomes known as a bomb thrower, there's going to be trouble."

It was at that point that Ruckelshaus revealed the approach he would take in his leadership of EPA. His response to that controversy set an example that was to be followed repeatedly in the subsequent actions of the agency. He did not pull back in the face of the criticism or wait for it to die down before striking out again. Instead, he forged ahead, confident that the tide of public opinion would support an aggressive approach. A few days after returning from Atlanta, Ruckelshaus requested the Justice Department to bring suit against the Armco Steel Company to stop polluting the Houston Ship Channel. A week later he requested a similar suit be brought against the Jones and Laughlin Steel Company to control its discharges into the Cuyahoga River in Cleveland. Additional enforcement actions were taken during that first month against other major companies. Ruckelshaus also stepped up efforts to deal with the huge volume of discharges by the Reserve Mining Company from its taconite ore plant at Silver Bay, Minnesota. All these cases spread the word that the EPA stood ready to get tough, even with the giants of industry.

Our first triumph came from our handling of an air pollution problem that plagued an area along the Ohio River in the vicinity of Parkersburg, West Virginia, and Marietta, Ohio. It had become one of the most notorious air pollution problems in the country, and our efforts were to produce a major breakthrough.

The Ohio River in that stretch along the border between Ohio and West Virginia forms a rather narrow river valley with rounded green hillsides rising 200 to 400 feet above the valley floor. The valley itself is partially protected from strong winds and tends to hold pollutants, which may accumulate to high concentrations. The sizable metal-processing and chemical plants that had been built along the river created pollution both from their manufacturing processes and from combustion of coal to meet their needs for energy. As early as 1951 a citizens' committee had been formed to fight air pollution problems, and in 1954 it obtained action by Union Carbide to install dust control equipment. Nonetheless, the air pollution grew worse as local industry expanded, and in 1964 a county health department complained that the Union Carbide plant was causing a major nuisance to local residents because of its emissions of heavy soot, which dropped black, carbonlike particles that left purple streaks when they became wet.

In 1967 officials from HEW convened an interstate conference to examine air pollution problems in the Parkersburg-Marietta area. Technical studies by federal officials had shown air pollution levels high enough to cause increased hospital admissions, injury to vegetation, corrosion of metals, and a greater number of deaths due to respiratory diseases. The main source of pollution was the Union Carbide metal-refining plant, which caused more than half of all emissions of particulate matter (smoke or soot) and well over two thirds of all sulfur dioxide emissions in the area. Analysis of samples of the soot disclosed significant amounts of chromium and manganese, which were attributed to the ferro-alloy process used at the Union Carbide plant.

Two years later the interstate conference reconvened. More recent studies had shown that emissions of particulate matter from the Union Carbide plant alone had increased significantly and that throughout the entire area they had increased by 29 percent. Predictably, complaints from local citizens focused on Union Carbide. A housewife recalled when its electrometallurgical plant began operations in

1952: "I shall never forget the first morning when I saw our clean Ohio Valley enshrouded with a plume of reddish or gray smoke or smog that brought visibility almost to zero." A doctor stated, "We have seen a marked increase over the past fifteen or eighteen years in respiratory diseases in this valley. I am talking about asthma, emphysema, acute bronchitis, all the allergies that pertain to people . . . We have to attribute this, I think, to air pollutants . . ." A minister estimated that he and his wife had spent more on doctors' bills for their children in the five months they had lived in that area than they had spent in the preceding five years. A school principal said that the children "made tracks in the black dust on the sidewalk as they entered the school although the sidewalks were swept the night before." A homeowner complained that although his home had been painted recently he already noticed a yellow discoloration caused by the pollutants.

The report of the federal officials who conducted the interstate conference concluded that the following adverse health effects had been observed in the conference area: "marked increases in respiratory diseases, including asthma, emphysema, acute bronchitis, and pneumonia; skin disorders; pulmonary fibrosis; sinusitis; allergies; headaches; eye irritation; and psychological depression." These were in addition to damage to vegetation, soiling and deterioration of property, and interference with outdoor recreation and family life. The federal officials recommended a comprehensive program to clean up the pollution. But Union Carbide refused to comply.

In the late fall of 1970, a series of severe air pollution episodes was bringing the inaction of Union Carbide to national attention. Stories describing the controversy between the company and the local citizens had appeared in the *New York Times*. At his confirmation hearings Ruckelshaus was challenged to do something to clear up this problem. He came back from the hearings and told us to get to work.

We quickly discovered the weakness of the cumbersome enforcement procedures contained in the 1967 Clean Air Act, which was then still in effect. Despite the company's undeniable failure to clean up its pollution, it was doubtful that EPA had legal authority to obtain court enforcement unless we could show that the pollution was creating a health emergency. Although our technical experts were convinced that the pollution had deleterious effects on health, we had no evidence to prove the type of sudden emergency the statute seemed to cover. We made a full search through the legal and technical features of the case, but the best idea that we could come up with was merely to send a letter to Union Carbide complaining of its recalcitrance and demanding that it take prompt action.

The air program staff prepared a lengthy letter recapitulating the background of the case and asking the company to explain what it proposed to do. When the draft letter reached my office, I pulled out my pencil to shorten the letter and toughen it up. The final letter referred directly to the recommendations from the interstate conference and commanded the company to respond within ten days, stating whether or not it would comply fully with those recommendations. It warned that unless a firm written commitment to meet these requirements was furnished within that period, EPA would begin enforcement action.

Ruckelshaus mailed the letter to Union Carbide and at the same time released it to the press. It was deliberately planned to put the company on the spot. We then waited anxiously to learn whether the company would yield to our demands or try to call our bluff. We had no way of knowing if it recognized the weakness of our legal authority or what we would do if it refused to comply. Day by day we waited, but heard nothing, and the suspense built steadily. Finally, on the afternoon of the tenth day, a staff assistant burst into my office, his face covered with a smile. "Union Carbide has sent in a letter," he exclaimed, "agreeing to all our demands!"

The case had enormous importance to the EPA enforcement program because of the psychological boost gained by an early and conspicuous success. It also revealed that effective publicity could supply much of the momentum of the early enforcement program. By tackling a serious problem and engaging the polluter in direct confrontation, we had brought to bear intense public pressure, which few companies could withstand. Again and again, the force of public opinion would overwhelm the objections of the company's lawyers and technical experts, who were clinging to defenses provided by the tortuous provisions of both the air and water pollution statutes.

Our next big case brought EPA into confrontation with the multinational giant ITT. It involved a large pulp mill of ITT-Rayonier located on Puget Sound in Washington. In many parts of the country (New England, the northern Great Lakes, and the Pacific Northwest) pulp mills have caused great amounts of water pollution. A chief step in processing pulp involves cooking wood chips in huge vessels to break down the structure of the wood and separate the fibers that will be used to make paper. Often an acid solution is used to aid the process. In later steps the wood fibers are cleaned by repeated washings. The waters discharged from these operations contain enormous quantities of organic waste that are separated from the fibers in the pulp, together with the lost acids and other pollutants. The ITT-Rayonier plant was one of the heaviest polluters. Several years earlier, federal and state officials had directed the plant to install waste treatment facilities to remove 80 percent of the pollution it was pouring into Puget Sound. The Washington State agency had tried to force the company to comply with those directives, but the company was adamant in its refusal. It claimed that the cost was too great and said there was no need for such expensive facilities since its pollution was thoroughly diluted once it entered Puget Sound. We viewed this as a clear example of recalcitrance, exactly the type of situation we were seeking for enforcement. At the end of January 1971, Ruckelshaus sent the case over to the Department of Justice with a request that it seek a court order against the company.

Public announcement of the suit brought representatives from ITT rushing to top officials at EPA and the Department of Justice in an attempt to negotiate an acceptable cleanup program. They quickly agreed to install all of the pollution control facilities called for several years before and also to remove 85 percent of the pollution, the higher figure now demanded by the state. At that point there appeared a division among the EPA ranks. EPA was conducting a general study of the pulp industry, and its preliminary recommendations were to require a 90 percent removal of pollutants. Several staff members argued that ITT-Rayonier should be forced to achieve the 90 percent level, since if the settlement with one of the biggest pulp mills in the Northwest required only an 85 percent reduction, it would be impossible to make other pulp mills meet the more stringent requirement. The argument was compelling, but the company insisted that it could not agree to such tight controls and would fight us through the courts if the government persisted in its demand.

The case culminated in a major negotiating session in Washington in late March. Representatives came across the country from our regional office, the state Attorney General's office, the Department of Justice, and the company. They met around a conference table at Justice. After hours of argument all details were resolved except the basic issue of 90 percent versus 85 percent removal. While the room was still filled with people standing by awaiting my decision, U.S. Assistant Attorney General Shiro Kashiwa telephoned to ask if I would not agree to accept the settlement at the 85 percent level.

I found myself faced with the question that recurs in every negotiation — whether to accept the best one can get by compromise or fight on into trial in hope of more complete success. Is the bird in hand in fact worth two in the bush? The State of Washington, the U.S. Attorney, and the head-quarters staff at the Department of Justice were all urging EPA to accept the settlement. They argued that it was a highly successful one, which would require a $20 million expenditure by the company and would result in a great reduction of its discharges. The technical staff of EPA resisted the pressure to abandon the 90 percent objective, however, and Bill Christian, one of the young lawyers on our headquarters staff, repeatedly stated that we must not set the precedent of backing down in a compromise and accept-ing a more lenient standard.

I had seldom been so baffled by the imponderables of a decision. I felt helpless to evaluate the sacrifice to our long-range program if I accepted the settlement, and I had no clear sense of our ability to achieve more after litigation. There was also sharp dispute over the effect of the 5 percent difference on the water quality in Puget Sound. My biggest handicap was that I had no firsthand knowledge of the scientific facts on which the decision depended. Many of the people working on the case knew much more about the matter than I did, but because they were in disagreement, I was the one who had to make the decision. Finally I called Kashiwa back and approved the proposal. Then I went downstairs and told Ruckelshaus that I had settled the case.

Even after the settlement was announced I continued to doubt whether I had reached the right conclusion. With the passage of time, however, it became increasingly clear that the choice was a fortunate one. Negotiations and litigation with other companies dragged on at an unconscionably slow pace, and it was more than two years before the agency adopted the 90 percent removal standard for pulp plants. In the meantime we enjoyed the benefit of another quick success. News of the agreement by ITT-Rayonier to invest $20 million in pollution-abatement facilities went a long way to encourage other companies around the country to commit major expenditures for pollution control.

During the first few months after EPA was formed it was the staff in Washington who developed proposals for enforcement. Murray Stein directed this work. Through the 1960s Stein had been the master of the federal water pollution enforcement effort, using as his forum the "enforcement conference." It was a unique procedure created by the early federal pollution statutes, and combined some features of a legal trial with others of a public hearing. While other officials had focused on research and technical studies, Murray Stein had seen, as Ruckelshaus was to see, that progress in fighting pollution could come about only through public support. He had mastered all the techniques for turning a technical hearing into an exciting public event. He would invite reporters to a bar for a drink and help them fill their note pads with newsy details. He would contact local citizens or conservation groups and arrange for their support. He would insist that his technical staff prepare a "stud horse report" on the worst pollution problems of an area and then write clear summaries, with charts and diagrams, that people could easily understand. He would rent hotel ballrooms and pack them with eager audiences. Then he would manipulate the order and timing of the presentations, needle the speakers, make wisecracks, coax information and promises out of corporate and city officials, and puff away on his long, thin, dark cigars.

Murray Stein had carried his road show across the country, drumming up public attention wherever he went and stirring up local officials. "We figured we couldn't stand to have more than four governors mad at us at once," he later observed. But Murray didn't worry about the enemies he made. He loved to travel, and he loved to be the center of the show. He knew the best restaurant in every city, and he had so many suitcases battered apart by airlines' baggage handlers that he finally bought a great aluminum-colored metal one that no amount of punishment could damage. Though he lived out of hotel rooms, he was having fun, and he was also doing more to further the cause of water pollution control than a truckload of technical studies could ever have done. In the course of his travels Murray Stein had learned where all the worst water pollution problems were, and when Bill Ruckelshaus wanted to move out with an aggressive enforcement program, Murray could tell him where to begin.

We soon concluded, however, that if the agency was going to run a strong program, we had to obtain active participation by our regional offices. Three months after EPA was created, Ruckelshaus summoned the regional directors of the water pollution program to Washington and told them to push ahead aggressively with enforcement cases. When the months that followed produced little action, I was puzzled. Slowly I realized that the biggest factor in the delay was simply the ingrained attitude of most employees in the agency.

Prior to EPA's creation the federal pollution control programs had focused on research, planning, grants, and technical assistance, and few of the people doing that work had any taste or training for the rough and tumble of enforcement. They felt inhibited by the opposition of their state agency counterparts, who resented the intrusion of federal officials. Then, too, enforcement work was complicated, and there were few lawyers or other staff in our regional offices with experience in handling such cases. All these uncertainties gave the head of each EPA regional office the uneasy feeling that an enforcement action might be improperly prepared. Because he knew the action would be attacked by the polluter and criticized by the state officials, he was tempted to forget the whole business and concentrate on grants and technical assistance.

These doubts would be allayed only if the feasibility of our enforcement plan could be proved within EPA itself. A group of cases in Massachusetts made that clear to me. After much prodding the Boston office drew up recommendations for eight enforcement actions dealing with two heavily polluted rivers in Massachusetts. The deadlines for installing treatment facilities were long overdue, and the Boston staff discussed the cases with state officials, who presented a variety of arguments against initiation of the eight actions. Negotiation produced an agreement that three would be dropped and the other five would be pursued. Our procedures next required the regional EPA staff to notify the dischargers in advance of issuing the formal notices of violation. The head of the Boston office insisted plaintively that the advance notification would create so much political pressure that we would be forced to back off. To set his mind at rest I arranged for Ruckelshaus to sign the violation notices first, and I promised to put the envelopes in the mail immediately after the contacts had been made. This would preclude our being stopped by political interference. We never had to repeat that special procedure, but until each regional office became experienced, the fear remained that political pressure would be used to block us and that the regional officer who had taken the initiative would be left out on a limb.

The early EPA enforcement program focused on water pollution because the Clean Air Act of 1970 had just been passed and during the next two years efforts were concentrated on setting the air quality standards and establishing the schedules for polluters to install control equipment. The deadlines for compliance had not yet arrived. In addition, the water pollution laws had recently been interpreted by the courts to permit suits against polluters. In several cities, especially New York, the U.S. Attorneys brought well-publicized suits to clean up notorious problems and obtained court orders imposing far more stringent requirements than the pollution control agencies had previously established. The federal law also allowed citizens to seek redress for their grievances about water pollution. It provided that one half of any fines collected might be awarded by the court to citizens who provided evidence of violations, and many citizens jumped at the opportunity. Two professors from the University of Pittsburgh, for example, went out in a small boat and collected samples of the discharges from dozens upon dozens of large industrial facilities in the Pittsburgh area. They demanded that the U.S. Attorney agree to bring suit at once against the polluters, explaining that at their request television crews from the local news stations were waiting outside his office for his answer. And Congressman Henry Reuss sent in a list of nearly 400 industries located in his home state, Wisconsin, demanding that we immediately sue them all.

Development of enforcement cases under these circumstances inevitably produced confusion. U.S. Attorneys around the country were excited at the prospect of becoming heroes by suing polluters, and demanded that EPA refer cases to them or provide assistance for prosecutions already underway. Citizen groups badgered EPA officials to take action against notorious polluters in their local areas. Meanwhile a small and inexperienced staff in each EPA regional office was attempting to sort through lists of plants that had failed to meet their various schedules, trying to establish priorities for enforcement action on a systematic basis. Headquarters was pushing hard for enforcement recommendations so that a national program could be set up, and state officials were urging that no federal action be taken at all. As a consequence of the conflicting pressures and uncertainties, the personalities of people in the different EPA regional organizations determined the actions that were taken.

The leadership to build a nationwide EPA enforcement effort came out of Chicago. Jim McDonald, the head of our program there, was one of the few lawyers who had been working for years in the water pollution program. His background gave him the essential combination of experience in both the legal and technical sides of pollution control, but the crucial factor in his success was motivation. Where others held back, he was ready to move ahead. McDonald quickly established an active and effective enforcement program in his region, which included the Great Lakes states, with their severe pollution problems. When enforcement leaders from other EPA offices observed his success, they were encouraged to follow his example. The rate of progress varied from one regional office to another, but gradually every office hired a small team of lawyers to supplement its technical staff and began to build up a caseload of enforcement actions.

Many of these changes took place far from public view, but they had profound importance. A new national program was evolving. The public demand for assertive action against polluters had made its first impact through individual decisions by leaders in top political positions, particularly Wally Hickel and Bill Ruckelshaus. Now the response to that public demand was being institutionalized. What had begun as a movement of protest was being established as accepted policy. Murray Stein's one-man show was being replaced by a new structure of government that would carry on an aggressive enforcement of pollution laws long after the early leaders had gone on to wage other battles.

There was one curious feature of the early EPA enforcement program: almost the entire emphasis was placed on beginning the actions. This meant either referring a case to the Department of Justice for litigation or issuing an administrative notice of violation. It was almost as though the mere fact of filing suit would end the problem once and for all, and if only we could sue all the polluters (as Congressman Reuss seemed to suggest) our environmental problems would be over. The difficulties of pursuing an action through to completion — achieving an actual cleanup program — seemed scarcely to be noticed, especially at first.

In a few cases the agency did achieve superb results. After long negotiations to work out consent decrees, we obtained court orders requiring major national corporations, including U.S. Steel, Jones and Laughlin, Du Pont, and Kaiser Aluminum, to clean up the pollution from several huge industrial plants. In most cases, however, the hopes raised by bringing suit against the polluter were destined never to be fulfilled. The negotiations or pretrial work had seldom produced any results before October 1972, when Congress enacted a new water pollution act. After that date the cases were held in abeyance until pollution control requirements could be established under the act's new procedures. Often the difficult work of reaching agreement on an acceptable cleanup program had not even started.

This lack of progress was doubtless due in part to confusion and inexperience among the government personnel. But a large part of the explanation was that litigation is almost never simple or quick. Nearly everyone exposed for the first time to the realities of court action is astonished at the length of court dockets, the complexity of pretrial procedures, the opportunities for delay by opposing counsel, the time and effort required for preparing cases for trial, and the numerous other difficulties in pushing a case through to adjudication. And after all this, there may be further delays caused by appeals. The result is that the life cycle of big court cases is measured not in months but in years. Moreover, once any pollution suit was brought, the wave of publicity quickly receded, and the corporate lawyers took over with no pressure from their side to hurry the case along, since expenditures for pollution control were postponed so long as the case dragged on in the courts.

The stubborn difficulty of these problems was revealed by

the proceedings against Atlanta, Cleveland, and Detroit, which Ruckelshaus had announced, amid such controversy, in his first official speech. Both in Atlanta and in Detroit the violation notices led to agreements on major construction programs; in Detroit alone the estimated cost of the construction was over $500 million. The facilities in these cities have provided treatment and control of serious sewage pollution problems. In Cleveland, however, it was another story. The flow of municipal wastes into the already polluted Cuyahoga River and Lake Erie had caused swimming beaches to be closed and had created obnoxious conditions. Public agitation had been building for years. An extensive municipal sewage system already existed, but sizable and costly improvements were needed. Of all the obstacles to be overcome, the most difficult was one that is almost never understood or appreciated by the general public — the need to develop the institutional arrangements to do the work.

In this case a single regional system had to be established to handle the sewage from the City of Cleveland and thirty-one separate suburbs. First there was bitter disagreement over the apportioning of costs between the city and the suburbs. Then a dispute erupted over who would manage the new regional authority (and thereby control the award of millions of dollars of construction contracts). After six fruitless months, I flew out with Murray Stein. We held a large public hearing to attempt to persuade the suburbs to reach agreement with the city, but deadlock persisted. At that point EPA issued violation notices to the thirty-one suburbs. But this struggle over the cost-sharing and management arrangements dragged on for more than a year and a half. It was resolved only after a county court, hearing a related case brought by the State of Ohio, imposed a building ban against new developments. Only then did it become possible to adopt a construction program to build the facilities needed to control the pollution.

The basic weakness of the early enforcement actions was that they were being initiated in areas where effective standards and pollution control requirements themselves had not yet been set. However aggressive the enforcement program, it could not be effective if it tried to establish these basic requirements by suing polluters one at a time. Nonetheless, vigorous enforcement did create an atmosphere in which pollution control had to be taken seriously by everyone. During its first two years EPA was to undertake over a thousand enforcement actions, and during the following two years the volume of enforcement activity expanded to cover more than five thousand additional actions. Within that time over $9 million in fines and penalties were assessed in a total of more than one thousand cases, including fines and penalties of $7 million paid by Ford Motor Company in a single case. Through these actions EPA became widely known for its tough and hard-hitting enforcement program. This was vividly illustrated in an emergency case that became one of our most dramatic achievements.

The scene was Birmingham, Alabama, one of the most industrialized cities in the South and one of the most severely polluted areas in the country. One of the few places in the country where iron ore, coal, and limestone are found close together, Birmingham early became a center for the production of steel. Huge sprawling complexes of steel plants and other heavy industry grew up alongside the Black Warrior River and, day in, day out, dark clouds of soot billowed forth from the blackened smokestacks. In normal weather the smoke moved across the valley, dropping soot on the houses and people, and then passed from view. From time to time, however, abnormal weather conditions would cause a large mass of warm air to hover over the city, trapping the cooler air beneath in what the meterologists label an "inversion." Occasionally these conditions would cause an accumulation of pollutants to reach high concentrations that posed a temporary but serious threat to the health of local residents.

To deal with pollution episodes that might occur around the country, EPA had established guidelines to identify pollution levels approaching dangerous concentrations. Exposure to pollution at these levels even on a short-term basis could exacerbate the problems of people with heart disease, asthma, emphysema, or other respiratory diseases. In many cases large increases in hospital admissions and in deaths have been recorded during short-term air pollution episodes.

On Friday, November 12, 1971, an inversion developed in the Birmingham area. The director of the County Health Department issued an advisory notice, suggesting that persons with a history of heart or lung disorders remain indoors as much as possible and avoid unusual exertion. That advice was withdrawn the next day as weather conditions appeared to improve, but by Monday the local officials had recorded pollution concentrations at disturbing levels. On Monday morning the County Health Department formally declared an air pollution "alert" and telephoned the twenty-three companies that caused most of the pollution, asking them on a voluntary basis to take steps to reduce emissions. That afternoon the monitoring stations scattered around the city registered several particulate counts at still higher levels, and at four-thirty a formal "warning" was issued. By Wednesday morning a light breeze suggested that the pollution might be ending, but the weather service forecast that the inversion would continue for another day. The warning remained in effect. County officials made a telephone check of the twenty-three industrial plants, including the biggest one of all, owned by U.S. Steel, to determine what steps had been taken to reduce emissions. That check revealed a partial, but incomplete, response to the earlier call for help.

Since Monday the Environmental Protection Agency had been maintaining telephone contact with the local officials, and on Wednesday EPA concluded that the seriousness of the episode demanded on-the-spot involvement 'by federal officials. Hasty arrangements were made to respond to the emergency. Darryl Tyler, director of the agency's Emergency Operations Control Center, flew in from the EPA offices in Durham, North Carolina; Bob Baum, the agency's top lawyer on air pollution matters, came down from Washington; and John White, director of the EPA Regional Enforcement Division covering eight southern states, came in from Atlanta. At a press conference that afternoon White explained that the federal officials were on hand to cooperate with the local officials and observe the situation but had not decided to take any formal action.

The EPA team gathered reports on the situation and made contact with the local U.S. Attorney. None of the lawyers had any familiarity with the mechanics of obtaining immediate relief from a court — the emergency provisions of the Clean Air Act had never previously been invoked — but they sat down and hurriedly began to write up a motion for a court order together with supporting affidavits. They also identified the judge of the Federal District Court, but by then the court offices had closed for the day. The emergency would not wait until the following morning, so they telephoned the judge at his home, and he gave them permission to meet with him there later that night if they felt it necessary. The federal team stayed in close touch with the local officials and examined each weather report as soon as it could be obtained. Those reports gave no encouragement that the inversion was about to end.

Shortly before midnight the federal officials concluded that they could not wait for a break in the weather to solve the health crisis for them. They drove out to the judge's home and submitted a formal complaint. It requested an immediate temporary restraining order against the twenty-three companies to stop their pollution. In the middle of the night in the judge's living room they presented their case to the court. A little before 2:00 A.M. Thursday morning the judge's questions were satisfied, and he signed the order. The federal officials rushed back to the courthouse and began telephoning the companies to explain the judge's order to amazed employees on the night shift and to call for immediate compliance. As each telephone call was completed, the companies promptly began to cut back operations and to send out the word to lay off employees for the next shift.

Tired, exhilarated, almost numbed, Bob Baum and John White trudged into an all-night café around three o'clock that morning for a cup of coffee. Whom should they meet there but Leon Billings, the brash staff aide to Senator Edmund Muskie and himself a principal author of the Clean Air Act. Billings had caught word of what was happening and had flown down that evening to observe the federal efforts during the next few days. Billings always talked tougher than anyone else in pushing for pollution control and was jocularly contemptuous of anyone working in the bureaucracy. Doubtless he half expected to keep book on the inadequate efforts of EPA so that he would be able to prod the agency later to take stronger action. He had just arrived and was startled to meet Bob Baum so late at night, but he was even more startled when he heard that the show was already over. Baum later reported, "When I told Leon Billings that we had already obtained the court order, his jaw nearly bounced off the counter."

On Thursday the weather began to change, and pollution readings dropped to safer levels. The court order remained in effect until the next day, when a cold front with strong winds and rain brought an end to the threat. The court then accepted a motion by the government to rescind the order.

News reports of the court-ordered shutdown of all major industries in Birmingham crackled across TV and radio, and banner headlines in newspapers around the country carried the story of the severe pollution crisis and EPA's prompt, effective crackdown. It is doubtful that any other single event so clearly demonstrated to the American public the power — and the willingness — of EPA to take strong action against polluters. For weeks afterward editorials hailed the agency's vigorous, purposeful response to the danger, and praised the forceful, independent action by Bill Ruckelshaus. The event was widely interpreted by columnists and political commentators as indicating that EPA was not subject to White House restraints and that Bill Ruckelshaus personally as Administrator had demonstrated his independence from external pressures.

Distracted by other work, I had not even heard about the air quality episode or EPA's involvement until the morning after the problem was solved. After being briefed as soon as I reached the office, I called Ruckelshaus, who was traveling in California. Because of the three-hour time difference, I was able to reach him in his hotel room before he had left for breakfast. I filled him in with a quick sketch of the problem and the action EPA had taken. Little did the editorialists and commentators realize as they heaped praise on Ruckelshaus for his resolute action that he too had known nothing about the incident until it was over.

CHAPTER 4

Caught in the Middle

THROUGHOUT THE COUNTRY the tide of environmental reform was running strong. Its force seemed bound by no limits. No one challenged the priority of EPA's efforts to achieve clean air and clean water. No one objected that the costs might outweigh the benefits. No one argued that the goals of environmental purity had to be balanced against other essentials of national life, such as economic production and employment. Industrial growth had been recognized as the source of ugly pollution, and a day of reckoning had finally arrived. As the agent of long overdue reform, EPA played the hero's role. One had to wonder how long the spell would last.

Ahead lay hard realities that would force EPA to make choices, to take positions that would draw attack. The most basic of these would be the conflict between the environment and the economy, and here the heat was first felt. Controversy broke out over EPA's handling of one of its first major enforcement actions, in a case that not only posed the fundamental question of which comes first, pollution control or jobs, but that illustrated the complexities of the interplay between politics and the formation of national policy. It raised the specter of improper White House influence over EPA's enforcement policy.

The case arose from one of the first of Bill Ruckelshaus's decisions — to launch an attack against the Armco Steel

Corporation for discharging pollution from its huge coking facility into the Houston Ship Channel. On December 9, 1970, just one week after EPA was formed, the Justice Department filed suit against Armco, charging that its discharges were "highly toxic and constitute an immediate health hazard." In striking at Armco Steel's plant on the Houston Ship Channel, EPA was striking at the heart of America's industrial pollution.

The Houston Ship Channel had long been one of the most extreme examples anywhere of environmental devastation. The reasons for this lay in a skein of factors involving the topography of the area, the history of its development, and the attitudes of its people. Houston is a huge, sprawling city, with a population of roughly two million people. The city's location is inland, some forty or fifty miles northwest of Galveston on the shores of the Gulf of Mexico. Yet Houston became a booming port city — the nation's third largest, trailing only New York and New Orleans — thanks to the Houston Ship Channel. Built back in 1915 by the U.S. Army Corps of Engineers, the fifty-two–mile channel in its upper portions follows the winding course of Buffalo Bayou, which flows through Houston from the west, and then for roughly twenty-five miles cuts directly across Galveston Bay. Along the upper stretch of the channel lies an enormous concentration of heavy industry — oil, petrochemical, wood products, food processing, and steel — the source of staggering amounts of industrial pollution.

Houston is a city of money. Capital of the nation's oil industry, it is likewise a center for many of the fortunes that industry has created. Houston is also a city of growth. One of the fastest-growing cities in the entire country, Houston proudly proclaims its lack of any zoning. In its pursuit of wealth, growth, and industrial development, Houston disregarded protection of environmental values. The symbol (and most flagrant example) of its willingness to sacrifice the environment in exchange for unbridled economic growth was the Houston Ship Channel. For decades the city's sewage was dumped into Buffalo Bayou, much of it raw or poorly treated, teeming with coliform bacteria from human feces, converting the ship channel into an open sewer. The mixture of domestic sewage and industrial wastes had destroyed virtually all aquatic life, except for the sludge worms feeding on muck on the bottom of the channel. The volumes of organic wastes had become so heavy that as they decomposed they often depleted the channel waters of all oxygen, creating anaerobic conditions. Oil, grease, acids, heavy metals, and toxic chemicals all poured freely into the lifeless, murky waters and drifted slowly down toward Galveston Bay.

Not surprisingly the effects of pollution on Galveston Bay were also detrimental. But the situation had been ignored for years by the people who mattered in the Houston power structure. The bay is not close to Houston nor does it possess spectacular beauty, though it is by no means devoid of natural charm. The flatlands and marshes that surround it form a fine habitat for birds and wildlife — once when I was flying over the area in a helicopter I spotted many large wading birds, including several roseate spoonbills in full flight directly beneath us, their pink plumage gleaming with indescribable beauty in the glow of a late afternoon sun — and the shallow waters throughout the bay provide excellent areas for fish and shellfish. During the 1950s and 1960s, however, harvesting of shellfish had been prohibited in large sections of the bay because pollution made the shellfish unsafe for human consumption. In fact, concentrations of oil and hydrocarbon residues had been found in oysters taken from areas that had not been closed. Fishkills frequently occurred in Galveston Bay, especially after heavy rainfalls flushed out the toxic pollutants collected in the ship channel and dispersed them into the bay.

This was the state — the result of neglect, abuse, and

degradation — of the Houston Ship Channel and Galveston Bay in 1970 when EPA was created. It was little wonder that when Bill Ruckelshaus asked for enforcement recommendations one of the first he received was that he bring suit against a big polluter pouring wastes into the Houston Ship Channel. It was also no surprise that the U.S. Attorney was able to present a persuasive case to the court. In June the case went to trial before the Federal District Court; and in mid-September the judge issued his decision, ruling entirely in favor of the federal position. He found that the Armco plant was discharging each day over 975 pounds of cyanide, more than 380 pounds of phenols, and between 6000 and almost 12,000 pounds of ammonia. He also ruled that the cyanide was lethal to shrimp and small fish of the species found in the Galveston Bay area downstream from the discharge point. The judge then issued a forceful order against the company — he prohibited any further discharge, effective immediately.

Important though this court victory was, it attracted little attention amid the rush and bustle of other events in Washington. Then, on Wednesday morning, September 29, 1971, I received a hurried request to come to the office of Peter Flanigan in the White House early that afternoon. I had seen Flanigan before only once or twice and did not know him personally, but his reputation marked him as a potentially dangerous critic of EPA. Flanigan had come to the White House from Wall Street and had brought with him the belief that the business of America is business. His own business career had been one of rapid success. He had been an investment banker, a partner in one of Wall Street's leading firms. He held a deep faith in the strength of a free market, viewed many activities of government with suspicion, and had little enthusiasm for the environmental movement or the vigorous approach of EPA. The most important attribute of Peter Flanigan, however, was his power. He was widely known as one of the most influential assistants to President Nixon. I could not help wondering why he wanted to see me.

I entered the West Wing of the White House that afternoon and presented my identification card to the guard at the desk. In a moment a man came to escort me upstairs to Flanigan's office. As we entered the small elevator that would take us up the two flights, I found myself face to face with John Whitaker. Whitaker, a good friend of mine, was our chief liaison with the White House, and I had seldom had any contacts with the White House except through him. He looked surprised at meeting me in the inner sanctum of the West Wing which, although outwardly a small and inconspicuous part of the White House, contains the President's Oval Office and the Cabinet Room and therefore is the true center of presidential power. Whitaker asked the obvious question: "What are *you* doing here?" When I answered that I had a meeting with Peter Flanigan but did not know why, John's expression changed to a frown. "I don't like his calling you over here and giving you a hard time," he said. Then after a pause he added, "That's what he's bound to do with the constituencies he represents."

The elevator door opened and we parted. The chance meeting fortified my confidence by reminding me that I had a friend in the White House. A few minutes later, I was ushered into Flanigan's office. I sat down and looked around. Obviously its prestige rested on its prized location within the West Wing. Not large as government offices go, the room seemed low-ceilinged and a bit cluttered. Its most conspicuous architectural feature was a support pole running from floor to ceiling smack in the middle of the room.

Smiling engagingly, Peter Flanigan sat behind his modern desk and pulled from a pile of papers a press release containing comments made by the President on a recent visit to Detroit. Flanigan proceeded to read at length from the

President's statement, which asserted his concern for the economy and his determination that American industry not be made "the whipping boy" of environmentalists. When he finished reading, Flanigan paused and looked across at me expectantly. Smiling back, I responded that I agreed fully with the statement. I felt relaxed but mystified about what would follow. Flanigan suggested that the President's statement should be distributed among all employees at EPA, and, his tone becoming slightly more taut, added that he would like to know if Bill Ruckelshaus saw any reason why that should not be done.

Flanigan then turned to a letter he had just received from William Verity, president of Armco Steel. Verity was not only a powerful figure in American industry; I had also heard that he was a well-known and influential leader in the Ohio Republican Party. His letter, dated the previous day and addressed to President Nixon, was as follows:

ARMCO STEEL CORP.
Middletown, Ohio

September 28, 1971

Hon. Richard M. Nixon,
The White House,
Washington, D.C.

Dear Mr. Nixon:

After hearing your comments at the Detroit Economic Club on the need for a sensible balance between the environment and jobs, and after personally hearing you tell us that industry would not be a whipping boy in solving our environmental problems, I was shocked by the actions of Mr. Ruckelshaus and the Justice Department in shutting down the blast furnace and coke ovens at our Houston plant.

It is inconceivable to me that your administration believes environmental problems can be solved by shutting down industry . . .

Ten days ago, Judge Hannay of the Federal district court in Houston handed down a decision requiring us immediately to cease discharging all cyanides, phenols, sulphides and ammonia into the ship channel. The decision did not give us any time in which to comply nor did it establish any acceptable minimums for these four materials. It has, in effect, shut down a major part of our operation there. The court order eliminated about 300 jobs in one stroke of the pen.

You should also know this ruling of the Houston court, if it were applied to others, would shut down not only all steel plants but also all chemical, oil, and many other industries, and every municipal sewage treatment plant in the country.

Armco is proud of its efforts and progress in environmental quality. In the past 6 years, more than $100 million of our shareholders' funds have been invested in air and water pollution abatement facilities throughout the United States . . . The company that has led the way in environmental improvement; the 300 men and women whose jobs are immediately affected; in fact, all employees of our Houston plant deserve fairer treatment than this.

Sincerely,

C. WILLIAM VERITY, JR., President.

Copies to: The Honorable John Mitchell, Attorney General; Mr. William Ruckelshaus, Administrator, EPA; Mr. Peter Flanigan, The White House; and Mr. Russell Train, CEQ.

Flanigan argued that our action was inconsistent with the President's policy and that it was up to EPA to conform. He added that Verity had a press conference scheduled for Houston the following morning and that I should try to straighten things out before then to avoid having the president of Armco Steel publicly attack the administration's policies in this area.

The whole matter took me by surprise. I had no specific knowledge of the status of the law suit, and I could argue only that it was a mistake to jump to conclusions until we had more information. I was alone at the meeting with Flanigan, except for two of his staff assistants, and had to make an immediate decision. I knew I could not disregard the challenge to EPA's enforcement program presented by Verity's harsh letter and Peter Flanigan's curt instructions.

My next move was a gamble. I invited one of Flanigan's assistants to come with me back to EPA while I explored the matter. I then telephoned Tom Harrison, our enforcement director in Dallas, and let Flanigan's assistant get on the line but did not alert Tom to his presence. It was taking a chance since I had no idea what Harrison might say, but I had calculated the chance to be worth taking. Tom explained that the agency did not want to shut down the Armco works but that we had been unable to negotiate a satisfactory abatement program. He said that if we could obtain an agreement, we would not object to the company's continuing operations while it installed the new facilities. Then Tom revealed something startling. He told me that the 300 employees allegedly thrown out of work in fact had been laid off several weeks before, when part of the plant had been shut down for maintenance repairs. The effect of the court order might postpone their rehiring, although rehiring was in doubt anyway, because of a weak market for the products of the plant. Flanigan's assistant was visibly impressed.

Later that evening the matter progressed several additional steps. Flanigan's assistant attempted to reach Shiro Kashiwa, Assistant Attorney General for Lands and Natural Resources, and in due course did talk to his assistant, Martin Green. He pointed out to Green the President's desire to avoid shutting down Armco's plant and suggested that something be worked out to stay the court order. Evidently Flanigan then talked directly to Verity and discussed the possibility of obtaining a stay. His assistant called Green back and explained that the government should join with Armco in requesting a sixty-day stay of the judge's order so that there would be time to reach agreement on an abatement program.

Overnight the lead role in the unfolding drama passed from Peter Flanigan to Martin Green. A more bizarre juxtaposition of personalities could scarcely be designed. Flanigan was suave, self-assured, high-powered, quick-acting and aggressive; Green was scholarly, cautious, deferential, and low-keyed. As a politically appointed top White House aide, Flanigan had easy access to the President and the responsibility for a wide range of important national policy issues. Green was a career government employee, who later explained that it was unusual for him to have any contact with White House personnel because, as he put it, in his ten years with the Justice Department "for the most part I have been a rather low-ranking Justice Department attorney."

In spite of these disparities the two men were pulled by circumstance into the Armco matter. Although they seem never to have spoken directly to each other, each played a critical role in the government's handling of the case. Flanigan, anxious to quash what appeared to him a flouting of the President's policy toward pollution control, devised on Wednesday night what he regarded as a suitable expedient. Green, receiving directions from an unusual source for handling a case in litigation, went into the office the next morning troubled not only over the irregularity of the procedures but also the proposed disposition of the case. From the government's viewpoint there was little advantage in seeking a stay of the court order in the absence of some concession by Armco. After attempting without success to clarify the Justice Department's position, Green telephoned attorneys for Armco to urge that they postpone the press conference. By that time, however, events had moved ahead, notwithstanding Flanigan's efforts of the night before. Down in Houston William Verity was going forward with his scheduled press conference.

Verity was the speaker at a luncheon meeting of several hundred businessmen at the Rotary Club of Houston. His remarks were direct and to the point. Verity praised President Nixon and attacked EPA. He said he had written to the President blasting the recent federal court decision against Armco. He indicated that high-level consultations were taking place concerning possible modification of the court order, and in particular he heaped praise on Texan John Connally, who was then Secretary of the Treasury and near the height of his power in the Nixon Administration. "I pray every night for John Connally," he told the audience. "If I could only have another son, his name would be John Connally Verity . . . At last there is reality in Washington, and it changes the entire outlook for the steel industry, and, more gratefully, Armco."

A week later, on October 6, the first negotiating session was held in Washington between Armco and the Justice Department (with EPA) to work out a settlement following the court order. Sharp disagreement broke out. The government lawyers assumed from their recent victory in court that Armco would finally be forced to agree to a satisfactory abatement program. Armco, in contrast, assumed that an agreement had been reached in the telephone conversation between Verity and Flanigan and that the purpose of the meeting was merely to work out details for the government and Armco jointly to seek a sixty-day stay of the court's order. Only then, its representatives declared, would the company begin to focus on cleaning up the pollution. Faced by this conflict, the negotiators could accomplish nothing. The meeting broke up in disagreement, confusion, and ill will.

Two days later a meeting was held in the White House office of John Whitaker to determine what approach should be taken by the government. Whitaker was one of six lieutenants on the Domestic Council staff who kept a watch over the activities of the federal departments. Their function was to resolve disputes and to make certain that officials acted in accordance with White House policy. Whitaker's sphere of responsibility included EPA. That gave him authority to define a White House position on this case even though the more powerful Peter Flanigan had already jumped into the middle of it. After hearing all sides Whitaker ruled that the discussions between Verity and Flanigan were not to be regarded as having established a government position. He said that the government should negotiate a pollution control program before agreeing to a stay of the court's order. With this clarification, the government lawyers went back to the bargaining table, but subsequent negotiating sessions produced little progress.

On October 19 an event occurred that was to transform the case and magnify its importance. An explosive article appeared in the Washington *Star*. "The White House has intervened on behalf of a company that is under a federal judge's order to stop dumping toxic wastes into a waterway," the paper charged. "As a result, apparently, officials of two federal agencies are now negotiating with the firm, Armco Steel Co., which wants to continue some dumping." The writer accurately described the status of the case and quoted an attorney for Armco as stating that they had gone to the White House "only when jobs were involved." The final paragraph of the article delivered a hammer blow. "During the 1968 political campaign, Armco's officers and directors contributed a total of at least $12,000 to committees supporting President Nixon's candidacy, according to a tabulation of donations compiled by the Citizens' Research Foundation of Princeton, N.J. They did not contribute to the Democrat's campaign, according to the tabulation."

The shock of the article was felt by the Justice Department and EPA. It immediately put us on the defensive. The next day the UPI wire service carried a story on the reaction

of Ruckelshaus, "denying improper White House intervention" and asserting that "he would quit if environmental
decisions are overruled because of political considerations."
Ruckelshaus said it was inaccurate to interpret the Houston
case as meaning that "what we've done is cave in to some
contributor to the Republican Party."

If the impact of the news reports on the image of the
agency was negative, its effect on negotiations of the case was
just the opposite. The morning after the Washington *Star*
article appeared, another negotiating session was held at the
Department of Justice. Tom Truitt, the tough trial lawyer
representing EPA, carried multiple copies of the clipping
into the conference room and spread them around the table.
"Gentlemen," he declared, "we're going to have to negotiate
an agreement that is above suspicion now." Armco stopped
resisting, the logjam was broken, and for the first time
negotiations began to move ahead.

On Capitol Hill reaction to the news stories was also swift.
Congressman Henry Reuss, watchdog supreme, sprang into
action. Reuss was chairman of a subcommittee of the House
Government Operations Committee, which dealt with conservation and natural resources. Its chief function was to
investigate government misconduct, a job Reuss performed
with intensity. He was a liberal Democrat and an ardent
conservationist. In 1968 he had exposed a near scandal — the
failure of the Interior Department to oppose the construction of apartment buildings on an area of marsh along the
Potomac River. The case had reeked of improper political
influence. In later hearings he had attacked the Justice
Department and other federal agencies for not taking bold
action against pollution and other types of environmental
damage.

Henry Reuss's mind was incisive. An honors graduate of
Harvard Law School, he had a trial lawyer's talent for
interrogating a witness. His questions were tough, probing,

often abusive, sometimes laden with blistering scorn. He insisted on detailed preparation, which was accomplished by his tenacious investigator, Phineas Indritz, and he knew how to follow up on any leads Indritz might uncover. Within hours after the October 19 issue of the Washington *Star* hit the newsstands, Reuss called a hearing for the next day to investigate the whole matter. He summoned EPA, Justice, and Peter Flanigan to testify. Just as quickly they fired back their responses, declining to testify on such short notice and on the ground that the matter was in litigation. There were pressures and counterpressures for scheduling a hearing, which was finally set down for November 5.

Meanwhile, negotiations between Armco and the government proceeded rapidly. Armco accepted the basic technological approach urged by EPA for control of its pollution discharges. It abandoned its argument for a deep-well injection system, which it had long sought to employ, and agreed to construct facilities to control and treat the wastes and incinerate the residue, as EPA had demanded. At last the parties had reached agreement, and they went back to the court with a substitute for the previous cease and desist order. The judge approved the abatement program on November 4 and ordered Armco to carry it out.

The next morning at ten o'clock I appeared in the hearing room of the House Government Operations Committee to testify for EPA on our handling of the matter. A stern Henry Reuss, flanked by several other Congressmen and a number of staff members, looked down upon us from his central position as chairman of the committee. To my right at the witness table sat Shiro Kashiwa, who would testify for Justice, and on my left was Congressman Bob Eckhardt, a representative from the Galveston Bay area. He would set the stage for the hearing by giving testimony on the severity of pollution in the Houston Ship Channel and the long-standing resistance of Armco against cleaning up its wastes.

There was a slight delay before the hearing got underway. I sat waiting, my fingers drumming on the table, and my memory raced back to the first time I had testified before a congressional committee. It had been nearly two and a half years before, when I had been with the Interior Department a scant three months. There, too, I had faced the inquisition of Henry Reuss, who wanted to find out why Interior had failed to comment on the effects of several proposed dredge and fill projects in San Francisco Bay. Reuss had caught me completely off balance by asking abruptly whether the Interior employee in that case had released a report on the projects "or did he suppress it?" I had answered that the term "suppress" was unfair, and there followed a long, heated argument about whether Interior had been required to release the report. When Congressman Reuss finally — with dramatic exasperation — had demanded a simple yes or no answer as to whether the report had been released, my statement that it had not seemed to be an admission of guilt. It had been painfully dragged out of a reluctant witness, and the event was celebrated in the morning paper with the headline INTERIOR DEPARTMENT OFFICIAL ADMITS SUPPRESSED DOCUMENT. The experience was etched on my memory. It had driven home a basic lesson: it was not so much the substance of what I had said that mattered as my evident reluctance in answering. If a witness appears to be hiding something, he is suspected of having something to hide.

As I waited nervously for the hearing to start, I knew it would be another sparring of wits, with Congressman Reuss again reaching for the headlines. The nature of the hearing was self-evident, it was adversarial and inquisitorial. Reuss's committee had the scent of blood. The circumstances suggested improper conduct. Their role as watchdog was to highlight the suspicious features of the case as sharply as possible. Our aim was to explain the basis for our action and justify its propriety. We had obtained agreement for an

ambitious abatement program from a company that had long
been recalcitrant, and the case had thus been an outstanding
success. Yet that agreement had released the company from
an absolute prohibition against making any discharge, and
the settlement had been reached after the company appealed to the White House. Those circumstances might give
rise to various interpretations. The way the facts would be
viewed by the audience (and reported by the press) would
depend greatly on how the testimony was presented. The
room was filled with suspense.

Congressman Reuss banged his gavel, and the hearing
began. Congressman Eckhardt gave his statement. Then I
read my prepared testimony, followed by Kashiwa, both of us
dealing generally with the government's enforcement program on pollution control. When Kashiwa ended, Congressman Reuss went directly to the Armco case. He moved
deliberately, setting his pawns out one at a time. He first
called on Kashiwa to confirm that Armco had been discharging 975 pounds of cyanide a day. He then quoted the court
order, which stated that cyanide "is one of the most toxic
elements known, being lethal to fish life . . ." and again
Kashiwa agreed. Next Congressman Reuss pointed to the
statement in the court order describing Armco's coke plant
as "patently antiquated from the standpoint of pollution
control." Another pawn had been placed with care. Reuss
then turned back to the original court order of September 17
and asked if it had not "forbidden" immediately — effective
at once — the discharge of those 975 pounds a day of
cyanide. He went on to ask if it was not true that the
November 4 order modified the prohibition and permitted
Armco to continue those discharges of cyanide until July 1,
1972.

Kashiwa by now was close to being cornered. He pointed
out defensively that both court orders were subject to the
condition of a permit to be issued by the Corps of Engineers,

but Reuss carefully took a detour to establish that the Corps of Engineers had not issued any permit and that item was therefore irrelevant. Reuss moved in to closer range. He asked whether Armco that day had resumed "discharging its daily 975 pounds of lethal, toxic cyanide into the Houston Ship Channel?" Kashiwa answered that he did not know, but in response to further questioning admitted that the company had the right to be making such discharges.

Reuss was poised, expectant. He referred to Congressman Eckhardt's testimony and asked whether it was correct that the president of Armco Steel had made contact with the White House concerning the court order. Kashiwa, squirming, responded, "I do not know. I do not know who Mr. Verity is. I have not met him." Reuss pressed: "You cannot corroborate, but neither can you contradict it?" Kashiwa answered, "That is correct." Reuss then asked whether Kashiwa knew anything about the statement that Mr. Verity had made contact with Mr. Flanigan in the White House. Again Kashiwa answered, "No, I do not know that."

Sitting next to Kashiwa at the witness table, I felt the tension rising in the room. There was one solution, quick, direct, and simple — get the facts out on the table, frankly and without delay. I raised my hand, caught Reuss's eye, took the microphone, and began to tell all I knew about the case.

I confirmed that Verity had sent Flanigan a copy of his letter to the President and that the two men had talked to each other by telephone. I explained that the Verity letter had caused concern not only in the White House; I myself had been disturbed by the charge that the court order would throw over 300 people out of work. Asked if I had a copy of the letter, I said that I had, and, for the first time taking the initiative away from Reuss, suggested that it be made part of the record of the hearing. I went on to describe all the facts of the case as I knew them. I finished by presenting a copy of the settlement order submitted to the court the previous day and, still on the offensive, requested that it too be included in the record.

The bubble was popped, the expectancy deflated; all the facts that might have caused embarrassment were freely set out. The possibility that EPA would be implicated in a political maneuver was reduced, but the danger by no means was over. There remained the matter of the propriety of Armco's appealing to the White House and the merits of the agreement we had entered into with the company. Reuss's attack was scathing. He argued that White House involvement in such litigation carried an implicit political influence: "This is akin to a 'fix.'" His anger flashed: "What I am suggesting is this: when the president of Armco or anybody else comes around to Peter Flanigan or Joe Doe in the White House in regard to a piece of pending litigation, he should be thrown out on his ear no matter how much he has contributed in campaign funds."

Reuss's charges placed me in an uneasy position. A government official in a sense is always in the middle, caught between the pressures from opposing sides in any controversy. He does what he thinks is best and then must defend his actions against whatever attacks are made. Instinctively I agreed with Reuss that Verity should not have gone to the White House. I also knew that Reuss's fierce attack would dissuade other companies from taking that route (as it did most effectively), which would strengthen our ability to achieve EPA's goals of cleaning up pollution. At the same time I knew that it was not a black and white situation. Nothing improper had actually been achieved as a result of Verity's letter, yet I dreaded the chance that a smell of scandal might linger over the case. This anxiety forced me, paradoxically, into becoming, at least in part, a defender of Verity's attempts to undercut our efforts. I pointed out that, although I disagreed with much of what Verity had done, I recognized the right of a citizen to complain to the President if he disagrees with action by the government. I emphasized that in his allegation that 300 employees were being thrown out of work Verity had challenged whether the basic policy of the President was being followed by Justice and EPA. Our most persuasive argument was that Verity had made his contact to the White House in the open, with deliberate publicity. "There was no element here of sneaking in the back door trying to obtain favoritism," I said.

The hearing ended in something of a draw. Reuss had made a number of telling points, the most trenchant being that the White House should not become involved in litigation by regulatory agencies. At the same time we had successfully explained our basis for entering the settlement agreement, and we had dissipated most of the suspicion attached to the White House involvement. The few reporters present evidently concluded that there had been no proof of misconduct, and the case was given no further publicity. I felt a great relief at having the hearing over.

Yet a number of questions raised by the Armco case are still unanswered. Does the President or the Administrator set the enforcement policy of a regulatory agency? When and how can a company properly challenge that policy? How can campaign contributors be kept from influencing regulatory decisions? How can small companies and individual citizens obtain the same opportunities to challenge actions as a large and powerful company? And when a government official is summoned to the White House to defend an action of his agency, how can he tell if improper "political influence" is involved and within what limits he should respond?

Beneath these issues, which dominated the hearing, were basic policy questions concerning the balance between the importance of jobs and the need for pollution control. The original court order would have required Armco to shut down operations in order to cease discharging pollution. EPA's approach, *after* an abatement program had been agreed on, was to allow the plant to resume operations. This permitted the pollution to continue while necessary control facilities were installed, but it meant that people's jobs would not be interrupted. In almost every instance, this approach was to be followed by EPA. At the time of the Armco case the policy had not yet been established. Underlying the questions of political interference that Congressman Reuss had pounced on was his suggestion that EPA should have shut down the Armco plant until pollution control had been achieved.

The attack by Reuss illustrated the force of political demands that pollution be halted immediately, almost without regard to cost or social impact. In the fall of 1971 public insistence on pollution control, then at its strongest, was used in attempts to shape government policy through political pressures, such as those applied by Congressman Reuss. Bill Ruckelshaus had won praise for taking forceful action against pollution. Yet he was being pushed to be even more aggressive. The Armco hearing was one example of the way in which this pressure was exerted. But a far more important trial lay just ahead.

CHAPTER 5

Confrontation with a Senator

THE CLEAN AIR ACT OF 1970 raised a host of difficult questions. Most of these were directed toward EPA as it developed regulations under the statute. Some of the questions were strictly administrative. Others arose because of the weakness in the scientific data on which decisions had to be based. Still others sprang from the fact that the statute, in setting the basic pollution control standards, neglected cost and feasibility, though these very real factors had to be considered by EPA when it formulated abatement programs. Environmentalists maintaining close personal contact with staff at all levels within EPA watched zealously over the program of implementation. During the fall of 1971 they began to fear that compromises by EPA would jeopardize achievement of the clean air objectives, and they transmitted these fears to their friends and supporters in Congress. In December we heard reports that the Senate Public Works Subcommittee on Air and Water Pollution, the "Muskie Committee," which had championed the act through to passage, would soon be holding oversight hearings. The subcommittee's purpose would be to explore charges that EPA was improperly softening the stringent requirements of the act. The hearings were to begin on February 16, 1972.

As the hearings were to make clear, there was ample basis for a congressional review. The Clean Air Act was designed to have a significant effect on the life of the country, but the scope and complexity of its provisions left many critical questions to be resolved during its implementation. That process had now run for more than a year, providing an extensive record to be reviewed. An inquiry by the subcommittee that wrote the bill thus was both customary and appropriate. At the same time, the hard questions raised by the Clean Air Act had broader implications.

Nineteen seventy-two was a presidential year, and in February Senator Muskie was a front runner for the Democratic nomination. A popular part of the Muskie record was his outspoken leadership of strong environmental controls, particularly his role as chief author of the Clean Air Act. EPA was on good terms with Senator Muskie, who was known to respect Bill Ruckelshaus, but a note of partisan animosity already existed between Muskie and the Nixon Administration with regard to the Clean Air Act. President Nixon had signed the act at a White House ceremony that included most of the law's congressional sponsors, with the conspicuous exception of Senator Muskie. Muskie had attacked the President for denying stronger support to environmental concerns. The oversight hearings gave an opportunity for the Muskie forces to fire shots at the Nixon Administration by publicizing any failings of EPA to carry out the Clean Air Act.

The hearings would place EPA directly in the path of the political crossfire. It had been EPA's job to resolve every uncertainty about the scope of the Clean Air Act. On many points Senator Muskie and the Nixon White House had conflicting views. These circumstances made Bill Ruckelshaus personally vulnerable. He had built his reputation for integrity and strong leadership by successfully walking a tightrope between the White House to which he was directly accountable, and the public, which expected of him vigorous environmental action. In any confrontation between Senator Muskie and the White House, Ruckelshaus would be on the defensive, forced to defend both President Nixon and his own record against any criticism that he had been soft when he should have been strong. The dangers inherent in these hearings were increased by election-year politics. In fact, the hearings were to produce the most ominous threat to Ruckelshaus's reputation that he would face during his tenure as EPA's Administrator.

The risks of embarrassment lay primarily in charges that the Office of Management and Budget was directing EPA to make many compromises, overriding recommendations of the agency's technical staff. President Nixon had created OMB in 1969 and had given it extensive power. Since its top officers were not confirmed by the Senate and did not testify before congressional committees, they could not be held accountable to Congress. Nixon critics charged that the growing influence of OMB represented a deliberate scheme to transfer power to an organization under the President's personal and exclusive control. The press had caught on to the controversy over the growing role of OMB, and charges of improper influence by it on so sacred a subject as pollution control were sure to set off fireworks.

Other recent events heightened the tension. In November 1971, the Senate had passed by an 86–0 vote a stringent bill to revamp the Federal Water Pollution Control Act. In the House Public Works Committee the bill had been sharply criticized and, with active administration support, the committee had modified it with numerous amendments. Senator Muskie had castigated the administration's position, charging both an intent to protect big business and a lack of concern for the environment. Ruckelshaus had responded publicly that Senator Muskie was "playing politics" with the environment issue. This attack boomeranged a week or two later.

Howard Cohen, a smooth-talking and assertive young man, had recently become the director of the agency's congressional liaison. Eager to please the staff in the White House,

Cohen distributed within EPA a detailed memorandum outlining the stand he proposed EPA take on a variety of bills then pending before Congress. The memo suggested bluntly that the purpose of the congressional program should be to make the President look good and that EPA should accept weakening provisions in the bills so that the objective would be achieved. The memorandum soon found its way to the congressional staffs on the Hill and to Ned Kenworthy, reporter for the *New York Times*, who gave it nationwide publicity in an article that amply quoted Cohen. Ruckelshaus, who had had no knowledge of the memorandum, was stunned. After an agonizing few days of evaluation, he called in the hapless Cohen and informed him that he was dismissed. This, of course, did not eliminate the problem. Although Ruckelshaus forcefully disavowed the policy set forth in the memorandum, the seeds of suspicion had been planted and there was nothing he could do to uproot them all.

Several days later I had a meeting with Leon Billings, Muskie's legislative aide. As we headed out of the New Senate Office Building together, I asked what effect he thought this incident would have on the reputation of Ruckelshaus. With unconcealed enjoyment, he quickly shot back, "It puts a nice little smudge on his forehead just after he accused Muskie of playing politics with the environmental issue." There was a slight pause as we walked along a couple of steps, and then Leon looked up again and asked, still in good humor, "After all, what else do people do in Washington but play politics with issues?"

The first three days of the hearings were designed to highlight charges that EPA had weakened the Clean Air Act. Ruckelshaus would be called to testify on Thursday and Friday, but first — to set the stage — a number of outside witnesses were called on Wednesday to lay out their criticisms and complaints. The first witness and the most important was Richard Ayres, director of a project on clean air sponsored by the Natural Resources Defense Council.

The Natural Resources Defense Council (now widely known as NRDC) is a small organization that sprang up in 1970 in conjunction with the arrival of the environmental movement. Financed partly by grants from the Ford Foundation and a few other prime supporters and partly by gifts of fifteen dollars or more from citizen members, NRDC has sometimes been short on cash but never on eagerness. Its two offices — one in New York City and the other in Washington, D.C. — are small and cluttered, with the makeshift air of a temporary operation. Young idealists, most of them under thirty, make up its staff. Yet despite these limitations NRDC has been a powerhouse within the environmental movement. Repeatedly its law suits and its reports have had a stunning impact on the development of national policy. With typical effectiveness, NRDC went for the jugular in these congressional hearings. Though Dick Ayres was a newcomer, with no personal standing in the field and virtually no experience in government, he proved to be the heavy hitter of the event. Ayres and his colleagues had tracked each step in the development of policy by EPA and the states on all the complex questions raised by the act. They had a clear position on every one of these issues and could fight for them with tenacity.

At the heart of the cleanup program under the Clean Air Act were the State Implementation Plans. The statute had required EPA first to set national air quality standards specifying levels that pollution could not exceed without having adverse effects on health and welfare. After these standards were issued in April 1971, all the states had to develop Implementation Plans. These spelled out the requirements for control of pollution by individual sources needed to meet the air quality standards. The State Implementation Plans had to be approved by EPA, and then they became enforce-

able under both state and federal law. Whole galaxies of legal
and technical questions were presented by the complex
requirements of these Implementation Plans, and evaluating
them was a herculean task. NRDC had kept pace with their
development, however, and had presented reams of criticism
on them to EPA. The Senate hearings gave them a chance to
set forth their complaints in public.

I did not attend the first day of the hearings, when Dick
Ayres testified, but several staff members from EPA were
present and gave us a report later in the day to help
Ruckelshaus prepare his testimony for the next morning.
Their report made it clear that Bill was in for a rough time.
Ayres had submitted a comprehensive evaluation of the
Implementation Plans and the issues they raised. He also
delivered an oral statement that was bitterly critical of EPA.
Said Ayres, "State Implementation Plans, which were to have
been comprehensive blueprints for new action, have mostly
become little more than weak-kneed apologies for each
state's present program." He turned his guns immediately
and with destructive force on the White House and OMB,
charging:

> The major blame for this situation must be placed squarely on
> the Nixon Administration. The White House Office of Manage-
> ment and Budget is reviewing in secrecy every major action of
> the Environmental Protection Agency. The public is com-
> pletely excluded from this review, but the most anti-environ-
> mental Federal agencies, such as the Commerce Department
> and the Federal Power Commission, appeared to have full
> access to it. These agencies, acting as spokesmen for industrial
> interests, have effective power to veto EPA's actions. Now
> becoming routine, OMB review is gelding the clean air amend-
> ments.

Ayres focused his attack on guidelines issued by EPA for
the states to use in preparing their Implementation Plans.

The purpose of the guidelines was to anticipate and answer many questions the states would face in developing their own requirements. The guidelines, in effect, were the framework for the whole cleanup program. On April 7, 1971, EPA had published the proposed guidelines in the *Federal Register* for public comment, and by June 28 had drafted a set of final guidelines incorporating many of the suggestions received. Then, according to Ayres, OMB had intervened and initiated an independent review. Subsequently, on August 14, "drastically weakened final guidelines were promulgated. Many of the best provisions of both the proposed and June 28 revised guidelines had been either weakened or cut entirely and additional weakening language had been added." Ayres charged that Ruckelshaus had "repeatedly and vehemently denied" that these changes had been directed by OMB.

Ayres argued that OMB had peppered the final guidelines with provisions requiring economic impact and cost-benefit factors to be considered. He charged that these provisions opened a loophole for polluters to avoid enforcement, at which point Senator Thomas Eagleton, one of the sponsors of the Clean Air Act, intervened: "On this question of an economic factor, I am as positive about this as a mortal can be, that was specifically written out of the bill . . ."

Ayres complained that OMB had cut out provisions to require a permit system for emissions and also provisions to require continuous monitoring and reporting of emission data by the polluters. He pointed out that the final guidelines allowed the states an entire extra year to negotiate compliance schedules with individual polluters and reduced the requirements for public hearings. Ayres criticized most of the Implementation Plans for not containing any adequate land-use and transportation control measures where required to control pollution and for not assuring that the standards would be maintained by dealing with the effects of

future growth. Finally, Ayres charged that OMB planned to
review the individual state plans before they could be
approved by EPA. Ayres asserted that the "questionable
legality and the disastrous impact of the OMB review process
I have described must be thoroughly investigated by the
Congress . . . We want to know who within the Administration forced the changes and who in EPA allowed them to be
made."

Senator Eagleton then dropped a bombshell — a flow
chart obtained from sources within EPA. The chart gave a
detailed outline of the review procedure to be used by EPA
in processing the State Implementation Plans; at the end of
the process was a specific reference to "OMB approval." This
underscored the accusations made by Ayres.

Taken alone, the testimony of Ayres on behalf of NRDC
might have had an almost devastating effect. It was not,
however, to be taken alone. Ayres was immediately followed
by Professor William Rodgers of the University of Washington. His testimony zeroed in on a problem that had
received widespread publicity: the abatement requirements
to be imposed on the copper-smelting industry. Rodgers
explained that in early 1970 several Western states (including Montana and Arizona) had been close to requiring copper
smelters to remove 90 percent of their sulfur emissions. At
that time a representative of the federal air pollution program had supported the 90 percent standard. After angry
protests by industry leaders, EPA had reversed that position,
and supported an approach urged by industry to set variable
control requirements based on daily weather conditions.
Rodgers attacked this approach as a "sorry strategy" for
controlling pollution, calling it "a lawyer's paradise of uncertainties in meteorological prediction, instrument calibration,
reading of ambient data and sorting out of SO_2 sources,
which has already bogged down thoroughly state and local
agencies."

By the time Rodgers finished, the clock was running late on the Wednesday morning hearing. Rodgers was followed, however, by three state officials who read brief statements, each of which contained further criticism of EPA's implementation of the Clean Air Act.

Bill Ruckelshaus was summoned to appear before the subcommittee at eleven o'clock that Thursday, leaving an hour for further critical testimony from the three state witnesses of the previous day. I rode up to the hearing with Ruckelshaus and entered the large hearing room a few steps behind him. When we arrived, the room was crowded with people and abuzz with chatter. Every seat for the public audience was jammed with reporters. On the raised platform behind the semicircular bench at the front of the room were half a dozen Senators, and perhaps a dozen or more staff members moved about behind them. The front of the room was ablaze with the glare of special bright lights, and several television cameras and other pieces of equipment had been placed at strategic points. Photographers snapped Ruckelshaus repeatedly as he made his way past knots of people and took his seat behind the witness table. For a fleeting instant I wondered what it had been like when the gladiators marched out to face the lions.

One of the protagonists in the confrontation was not present. Senator Muskie was in Florida on a campaign trip. Senator Eagleton presided in his stead. A Democrat and former Attorney General of the State of Missouri, Tom Eagleton had been elected to the Senate only three years before. Leon Billings hovered at Eagleton's left ear and whispered information to him. Billings had great influence, especially in light of Muskie's rising presidential prospects, and I wondered what clever strategems he had dreamed up for this occasion.

Finally Senator Eagleton banged the gavel and brought the hearings to order. He set the tone in his very first comments, pointing out that previous witnesses had brought strong supporting evidence to charges that serious compromises had occurred in implementing the Clean Air Act of 1970. He summarized eight separate counts of apparent failure by EPA to fulfill the directives of the act and then called on Ruckelshaus to speak.

Ruckelshaus was equally direct in his response. He read only brief excerpts from his lengthy prepared statement and then addressed the issue of the day. "Let me direct my attention to charges that EPA has given up control of decision-making regarding the Clean Air Act to the Office of Management and Budget . . . That charge is categorically false." Ruckelshaus referred to the changes in the guidelines, and then made a striking and unexpected counterthrust. To the evident surprise of Senator Eagleton, he presented a letter, sent by Senator Muskie the preceding May, that questioned some of the specific directives in the guidelines EPA had proposed on April 7. Ruckelshaus quoted from the Muskie letter, which said, "Local conditions will require flexibility" and recommended that each state be "free to choose the most effective control strategy." Ruckelshaus agreed that one could argue that, in modifying the guidelines to follow the recommendation of Senator Muskie, he had "caved in" to the chairman of this subcommittee, but, he protested, "the final decision on the issuance of those regulations is mine and [almost shouting] mine alone."

Senator Eagleton referred to the flow chart he had introduced the day before, which indicated OMB approval as the final step before publication of the plans or standards. Ruckelshaus met the issue head-on with a flat denial that the chart set forth the policy of EPA. He said that with eight thousand employees in the agency mistakes were sometimes made and that the "OMB approval" at the end of the flow chart was "simply false." He explained that OMB would sit on a committee to review the cumulative effect of all State

Implementation Plans but would not approve the individual plans themselves.

Senator Eagleton shifted his grounds. He asked about a change in the guidelines reducing requirements to include rigid emission limitations in all State Implementation Plans. Ruckelshaus gave answers that were convincing and unequivocal. Senator Eagleton said that he would get back to the emission limitations problem later; this attack seemed to be losing some of its steam.

At that point, Senator Jennings Randolph of West Virginia, the conservative senior chairman of the full Public Works Committee, interrupted to ask several questions and to express his approval of the EPA approach, commenting, "Mr. Ruckelshaus, I have a very high esteem for you." And then, "I like what you said," and later "In fact, I have much confidence in you."

In the psychology of the confrontation the Randolph comments blunted the thrust of Senator Eagleton's interrogation, but Eagleton returned to the attack. He again homed in on the role of OMB, making the point that OMB got a final crack at the guidelines after the close of the public comment period. Ruckelshaus answered that OMB did not get any final crack at the regulations and that although he had received comments from many sources the final decision had been his. Senator Eagleton returned to the issue of the emission limitations and asked several questions that Ruckelshaus handled with ease. After several exchanges, the Senator stated with some exasperation his belief that an emission limitation was required in every Implementation Plan. Ruckelshaus asked whether this was true even though there might be no violation of the air quality standard. A ripple of laughter ran through the room. Tom Eagleton glanced up, a look of wonder crossing his face when he found the audience was laughing not with him but with Ruckleshaus. It was obviously the turning point.

When the hearing ended a few minutes after twelve, it was clear that Ruckelshaus had achieved an impressive triumph. He had entered a room filled with suspicion, criticism, and the expectation that he was about to be badly embarrassed. Instead, he had answered the charges persuasively. He had successfully defended both EPA's reputation and his own. People crowded around Ruckelshaus with admiration as he slowly began to work his way out of the room.

Ruckelshaus's success on that first day of his testimony demonstrated the value of skill and preparation. He had known more about the issues than Senator Eagleton did and had used his knowledge effectively. In the oversimplification of issues that is so common in political debate, the emphatic statements by Ruckelshaus that he had made the final decisions carried the day. Beneath the surface, however, was a more complicated reality. The critical fact that slipped past Senator Eagleton was that in the complex operations of a government bureaucracy the final decision often is not the most important one. Before a major regulation assumes its final form, dozens of preliminary decisions are made, which mold and change the end product. The establishment by OMB of procedures to review proposed EPA regulations, therefore, gave it an important influence over EPA's policies, even though Ruckelshaus retained control of the final decisions. That intervention by OMB reflected political pressures quietly exerting their force against the strong environmental requirements. Because of the way the hearings developed, the full extent of those pressures had not been revealed to the public. But another day of testimony was still to come.

Ruckelshaus returned to the hearing room at ten o'clock the following morning. This time the atmosphere was entirely different. Gone were the floodlights, the television cameras and photographers, the overflow crowds, and the sense of tense drama. To outward appearance, it was just another day of hearings. Yet to those familiar with such proceedings, there was an atmosphere of tense concentration. Senator Eagleton had another chance, and it soon became apparent that a good deal of homework had been done overnight. The Senator had dates and facts and documents clearly set in his mind, and was obviously intent on nailing EPA.

Alternately questioning Ruckelshaus and Dr. John Middleton, head of the EPA air pollution program, who was sitting beside Ruckelshaus, Senator Eagleton laid out the full chronology of the guidelines for the State Implementation Plans from their publication in proposed form on April 7 through the revised draft approved by Dr. Middleton on June 28 and their final issuance on August 14. Eagleton pinpointed the changes made between June 28 and August 14 and declared that the guidelines had been "distorted" and "emasculated" by those changes. On each subject he crisply presented his information and his charges and then moved on to the next item. Largely by-passing the issue of whether OMB or Ruckelshaus had made the final decision, Senator Eagleton this time did establish effectively that several important points of the guidelines had been changed between the June 28 version and the August 14 final form, and that the changes were all in the direction of loosening or relaxing the requirements.

Sitting in the audience of the hushed hearing room and exchanging occasional glances with several reporters at the press table a short distance away, I felt the sting of Eagleton's charges. His interrogation then shifted to the emission limitations for copper smelters and the change in EPA's position with respect to the Montana plan. Senator Eagleton proceeded step by step — through each piece of correspondence, meeting, or telephone call — to trace the chain of events from the original testimony supporting the 90 percent limitation in the Montana plan to the eventual letter disavowing that testimony. The implication was that the change occurred as a result of White House intervention, though Ruckelshaus denied emphatically that the White House had dictated the change.

The hearing on Friday was more lengthy and more contentious than that· on Thursday. It ended with charge and countercharge. Eagleton proclaimed that Ruckelshaus had failed to persuade him that EPA had not changed its guidelines and weakened its enforcement of the Clean Air Act in response to industry pressure exerted through the White House and OMB. Ruckelshaus concluded with an emotional statement that in a society afflicted with mistrust of our institutions the accusations of the subcommittee would make it more difficult for EPA employees to function effectively. Senator Dole labeled the charges by Eagleton election-year politics and said that on conclusion of the hearings — or trial — he found the defendant not guilty.

Although the television cameras had not returned for the Friday hearing and the audience had fallen off, the hearings were reported at length in the *New York Times,* the Washington *Post,* the Washington *Star,* and many other newspapers. The controversy over charges of misconduct or improper White House influence upon decisions by the agency dominated all the accounts. The stories were not slanted against Ruckelshaus or the agency, and readers were made aware of the element of election politics, but the net effect was that serious questions concerning the integrity of EPA's performance had been brought to public attention. It was the first time that Ruckelshaus or EPA had been under heavy fire. The reporter for *Time* magazine, Sam Iker, commented to me later that at some moments during the hearing on Friday Bill had seemed "beleaguered" and "did not have convincing answers to the questions that were raised."

Frequently after those hearings Ruckelshaus was asked at press conferences whether his decisions had been dictated by the White House or whether he had "caved in" to industry, but the agency's record of action tended to counteract such skepticism. As month after month passed, EPA's energetic enforcement program, its achievements in establishing firm regulatory requirements, and its positions on legislative issues pending before Congress, together with the strong public statements and attractive personality of Bill Ruckelshaus, laid to rest nearly all doubts as to the vigor and integrity of EPA.

The oversight hearings and Senator Eagleton's critical blast had threatened to undermine the high respect commanded by Ruckelshaus and the Environmental Protection Agency, but they could not destroy it in a single attack. Public attitudes are seldom shaped by one incident; rather, they are consequent on a gradual accumulation of observation and comment. For most people, individual events become part of a general impression and slip quickly into the subconscious. On the whole, EPA appeared as the embodiment of positive government action to solve serious problems of pollution. EPA was an exemplar of forceful leadership. That was what the public clearly wanted, and the agency proceeded through 1972 with broad and powerful public support.

The hearings conducted by Senator Eagleton must be assessed not only through their revelations of previous actions of EPA but through their impact upon subsequent actions. That impact was substantial. By holding Ruckelshaus strictly accountable for any softness in EPA's regulations, the hearings exerted pressure on the agency to take a firm stand when dealing with future cases. The packed attendance at the hearings and the close attention by the press were signs of the continuing public insistence on vigorous environmental programs. They made it clear to Ruckelshaus — and to everyone else — that any tampering with the strict commands of the Clean Air Act would not be tolerated in the politics of 1972.

The story of actions by the federal government to meet the environmental crisis, therefore, is not the story of a few courageous leaders battling against fearsome odds to win reforms. It is instead a story of how the government responded to a public that demanded change. Government officials work in an adversarial world of challenge and critical comment. They may fight for their own convictions, but they also must react to the pressures that surround them. In the aggregate, the course of government action is controlled by deeper political forces. Government officials are responsive — and they must be responsive — to those deeper forces. The record of action on the environmental issue demonstrated that responsiveness. It also showed the irresistible power of the environmental movement.

To the Environmental Protection Agency the explosive events of the environmental crisis bore a special importance. They occurred during the formative period of the agency's life and shaped basic attitudes and approaches deep within its bureaucracy. The inclination of the idealists who flocked to EPA at its formation was to demand far-reaching changes to solve environmental problems. That inclination was reinforced by instances in which Bill Ruckelshaus took decisive action and by the political pressures exerted against the agency. A time would come when that approach would bring criticism against EPA for being "overzealous" and "unreasonable," but in 1972 such a prospect seemed remote. Tested by the prevailing public attitudes, the only danger seemed to be that EPA might not be ardent enough.

During the upsurge of environmental concern, the federal government set a policy of cracking down on pollution. It made sweeping commitments to achieve clean air and clean water. These commitments raised a fundamental question: whether there would be a sufficient follow-through to achieve the goals so eagerly adopted. An examination of what has happened in the subsequent years will tell a great deal about how successful our government can be in solving serious national problems.

First, however, it is important to look more closely at how our government actually operates. Government policy in any field is established by a complex set of mechanisms. They include the bureaucracy of the agency running the federal programs and its relations both with the White House and with the Congress. An analysis of the struggles and controversy that dominate these relationships will illustrate why it was so critical to the environmental movement to possess a broad base of public support.

The dynamics of government operations arise from the interplay of politics in setting government policy and the hard realities of running government programs. These are best seen by looking behind the scenes at a single government program, one that became the cornerstone of efforts to control industrial water pollution. To pick up the story of that program, we must turn back in time to a meeting held in November 1970, before EPA had started operations and just a few days after Bill Ruckelshaus had been nominated to be its first Administrator.

PART II

The Gyrations
of Government

CHAPTER 6

An 1899 Law Springs to Life

IT WAS CLOSE to eleven o'clock on that November morning of 1970 when I turned the corner of Pennsylvania Avenue across from the White House and headed up the sidewalk of Jackson Place, the one-block street running alongside Lafayette Park. The bleak gray clouds overhead and a damp breeze gave a slight chill to the late autumn day, but I felt warmed by the brisk walk from my office at the Interior Department several blocks away. I glanced at my watch, wondering if I might be late, and hurried along Jackson Place past several handsome red brick row houses. Partway down the block I turned up the steps of one of these houses and entered the office of the Council on Environmental Quality.

CEQ, as the council had become known, was still in its first year of existence but was in its heyday. It was a small staff office created to advise the President on all environmental issues, and the emerging power of the environmental movement gave it strength to push for changes in many federal programs. It had taken command of presenting the President's environmental program to Congress the previous spring and was putting together a set of ambitious proposals for the coming year. I had followed these activities of CEQ with a close personal interest because its chairman was Russell Train, the man who had first hired me to come to Washington. That had been nearly two years before, while he had still been the Under Secretary of the Interior. During the past year Russ Train had become a national figure, and what he had to say in policy debates within the administration was listened to with respect.

When I walked through the front door at CEQ I found that many others had already arrived and were greeting each other in the crowded reception area. We filed into the library, a long narrow room on the first floor set up for the conference. It was an attractive room, its walls lined with bookshelves, and with handsome brass chandeliers hanging from the high ceiling. About two dozen of us took seats around the long table. I found myself at the foot of the table; at the opposite end, presiding, was Russ Train. He was my friend and a man I respected, but I knew I would differ with him that morning.

In retrospect that meeting stands out as a critical moment in the evolution of our national program for water pollution control. It was the occasion when the federal government first committed itself to creating a bold new system requiring permits for all industrial discharges. Ultimately that system would engage the efforts of thousands of people. The effects of its implementation would be felt in board rooms of nearly every major industrial corporation. And it would change the nature of pollution control efforts on every stream in the country. Yet virtually no one outside the government — and very few inside it — had any knowledge of the proposal to be debated that day. And even those few of us who attended the meeting could not foresee how the program would finally develop.

The proposal would require every industry discharging any wastes into public waterways to obtain a permit from the federal government. The permits would specify the abatement requirements for controlling the pollution of each discharger. The idea was simple, but its background was odd and confusing.

In the days of President McKinley, Congress enacted the

Refuse Act of l899, which prohibited any deposit of refuse into the navigable waters without permission from the Army Corps of Engineers. For decades this was understood to apply only to refuse that might obstruct navigation, but in the early 1960s the Supreme Court ruled that the act also prohibited discharges of liquid materials. A few years later U.S. Attorneys began to use the law to sue polluters. Then came the lightning bolt — Walley Hickel's invoking the Refuse Act against the Florida Power and Light Company. Hickel's action brought national attention to this method for bringing suit against industrial polluters. The Refuse Act offered an opportunity to by-pass the whole slow-moving administrative machinery established several years before by the Federal Water Pollution Control Act. Since the Corps of Engineers had never issued permits for water pollution discharges, every industry discharging wastes suddenly found itself in violation of the law. The Department of Justice began to gear up for an active program of court suits against major industries to require adoption of cleanup programs. The realization that confusion would attend any effort to establish consistent requirements for all of American industry through individual law suits soon prompted another idea: polluters should be required to obtain government permits.

During the summer of 1970 two separate parts of the federal bureaucracy began a quiet campaign to elicit support for a permit program. The Corps of Engineers, ever ambitious, hoped to expand its activities in water management and enter the field of water quality control. In addition, the Federal Water Pollution Control Administration (which was then still in Interior but was about to be shifted to EPA) saw the program as an opportunity to tighten its control over industrial pollution. It wanted a method to impose rigorous limitations on the pollution discharged by plants in each industrial category. Officials from both agencies promoted the idea and found supporters in Congress and in the executive branch. In the early fall Russell Train publicly endorsed the concept of a new permit program in testimony before a congressional hearing.

Because the permit program would be based on the 1899 statute rather than on new legislation, the decision to create the program lay within the power of the President. The profusion of presidential actions, however, defies the grasp of any one man. Like most "presidential" actions, the real decision in this case would be made by a group of subordinates who seldom if ever even talked to the President. If enough support for a proposal could be lined up among key officials in the affected departments and within the White House staff, a recommendation would move upward through channels and the President's signature would appear on the needed Executive Order.

Life in the government is a series of meetings. Constant communication is the medium through which the merits of proposals are debated and major decisions are made. Promotion of a new program is a battle of ideas, and the meeting at CEQ would be the decisive testing ground. Russ Train's support gave the proposal a tremendous boost, especially since he would preside at the meeting. Nonetheless, many others would have a say. Seated around the table were representatives from several federal agencies, each of which would support or oppose the new program according to the manner in which its interests were affected. John Whitaker and other staff members from the White House and OMB were there for the debate. In addition, seated on Train's left was a man whom most of us had never seen before. He was Bill Ruckelshaus, just appointed a few days before to head the new Environmental Protection Agency, which would be chiefly responsible for running the program.

Russ Train opened the meeting. He welcomed Bill Ruckelshaus graciously. Next, he outlined the proposed new permit program and described its advantages. Then he looked down the table directly at me and asked if I had any objections. I did. I knew that my position might not carry much weight since I was representing the Interior Department, which was about to lose the water pollution program, but I was convinced that the proposed new program presented many practical problems and that they had not been considered thoroughly. I predicted that it would be exceedingly difficult to develop pollution control requirements for the various industries and then apply them to individual plants. Finally, I argued, running so complicated a program as a joint venture between the Corps of Engineers and EPA would lead to chaos. Because the program would become the cutting edge of EPA's pollution control effort, it was absurd to give the Corps of Engineers the authority to issue the permits. When I finished, a friend of mine sitting next to me, Doug Costle, drew a picture of a bull's eye and slipped it to me.

It was quickly apparent, however, that I was almost alone in opposing the program. The Department of Justice expressed fears that the new system would prevent it from using the Refuse Act to bring law suits against polluters, but everyone else supported the proposal. I listened as Dave Dominick, head of the Federal Water Pollution Control Administration, said it would help greatly to clean up pollution. The Army Corps of Engineers, represented by one or two civilians and two colonels in military uniform, urged that the program be adopted. To my surprise even the Department of Commerce came out in favor; — its representatives said the program would set requirements more equitably than the current system of individual law suits. It was obvious to me that the proposal's advocates had achieved very nearly unanimous support. As the consensus became clear, the federal government gradually, even subtly, crossed the dividing line between debating a proposal and implementing a decision. After a while the discussion shifted to the way in which the program would be announced. No vote or formal action had been taken, but the matter was decided.

When the meeting adjourned I caught up with Bill Ruckelshaus in the hall and introduced myself, and chatted for a few minutes. I pointed out that, unlike everyone else who was urging that we rush ahead, he would have to defend the program if it later ran into trouble. I had no inkling then of the ironic twist that fortune would take; because my critical analysis had caught the attention of Ruckelshaus, he would hire me as one of his Assistant Admininstrators and put me in charge of starting up the program. For the next few years I was to be directly responsible for establishing the new national permit system. It was to give me an A-to-Z exposure to all the practical problems and political obstacles in putting a major program into operation. That experience taught me how hard it is, and how long it takes, to build and run the machinery of government.

On December 23, 1970, I went over to watch Russ Train announce the establishment by the President of the new permit program. Flanked by Ruckelshaus and Bob Jordan, General Counsel of the Army, Train stood before the microphones in the White House press room. It was the first time I had attended a White House news conference, and from my position amid a small knot of assistants to the right of the rostrum I looked out across the room. It was difficult to see through the glare of the floodlights, but soon my eyes adjusted to the brightness, and I noted the scene. The room was deep and narrow, and seemed hazy with smoke in the glare of the lights. An odd assortment of furniture — sofas, easy chairs, and other seats — was scattered casually about. Three television cameras on tripods dominated the foreground and partly obstructed vision toward the rear, where many reporters were sitting. The podium was modest, elevated only a few inches above the floor, though backed by blue curtains, which would probably suggest in the evening telecasts a grace and elegance quite absent from the room itself.

My observations were interrupted by Train's presentation and the questions it sparked. I was so naive as to expect that announcement of a new program to curb industrial pollution would be warmly welcomed by the press. I was later to learn that nothing is warmly welcomed by the press. In this instance the reporters' cross-examination concentrated on the honesty of the men running America's industry. One pair of questions was asked over and over: How could the government be sure that the discharge reports filed by the industry would be honest? Would we throw the businessmen in jail when we found that they had lied, as we surely would find if we could be counted on to look? Yet the skepticism implicit in these queries did not come through in the newspaper accounts the following day. They accurately reported the start of the new program, which now was off and running.

Immediately, however, a storm of controversy crashed over the program. Industry was aghast at the sudden imposition by the President of a system involving permits, penalties, and demands for information. Environmentalists rang the alarm that the permits would be too lax. On Capitol Hill the committees responsible for the federal pollution legislation were chagrined at the creation of a new federal program initiated without congressional approval. To crown it all, there were no firm answers to basic questions concerning the standards by which the program would be administered. Receiving fuzzy answers to their most obvious questions, many people felt they were getting double talk and accordingly feared the worst. For several months harsh criticism swirled around the program.

The uncertainties and criticism made it essential to develop quickly the nuts and bolts of the system. An application form had to be prepared and distributed so that it could be completed by each industrial plant. Roughly forty thousand applications were expected, and they would be due by July 1. Working together with the Corps of Engineers, we needed to lay out ground rules for processing the applications. In fact, a complete set of procedural and administrative regulations was needed. There was much to be done — more than any of us could anticipate at the time.

The most elemental dispute was over the standards to be applied. Would EPA apply the water quality standards already established by the states or would we impose new requirements? Although state agencies were livid over the prospect that the permits might supersede their requirements, environmentalists insisted that the state standards were hopelessly inadequate. More problems crowded in upon us. Several questions arose over whether various government agencies, both federal and state, would have a chance to review the permits before they were issued. Others concerned the rights of citizens to participate in the review. These stressed the need for public disclosure of data submitted by the companies and for public notice and public hearings on individual permits. As each of these demands was resolved, the complexity of our procedures multiplied.

We held dozens of meetings to thrash out the regulations, some strictly between EPA and the Corps, others involving other federal agencies, outsiders, industry, or environmentalists. The issues were sharpened at congressional hearings by a special panel under Senator Philip Hart and Congressman Reuss, two of the strongest environmental protection advocates on Capitol Hill. They vigorously criticized many features of the program, especially its reliance, to however small an extent, on state agencies or on existing water quality standards. Emphasizing that the permits would be nothing more than a "license to pollute," Congressman Reuss labeled them "tickets" — and asked me derisively, "When will you start giving them out?"

While environmentalists were complaining that our requirements would be too flexible, those affected by them objected that they would be too rigid. Some problems were completely unexpected. One, for example, concerned the application of the permit requirements to farmers. The program had been intended to deal only with industrial wastes. Municipal wastes were specifically excluded by the language of the Refuse Act, and nobody had dreamed that run-off from farms or animal feedlots might be covered. But someone discovered that the terms of the Refuse Act might be interpreted legally to include agricultural discharges.

The news spread instantly among the farming interests, and they reacted immediately and in force. Calls came in from everywhere, and before we knew it the House Agriculture Committee had scheduled hearings on the matter. Frantic meetings quickly followed. We all knew that EPA and the Corps of Engineers were not equipped to handle applications from thousands upon thousands of agricultural sources, and, besides, curbing agricultural waste was not the purpose of the program. Just before I and several others were scheduled to testify at the hearings called by the House Agriculture Committee, we made a fast decision to exempt all agricultural discharges except those from the largest feedlot operations. Looking up from the witness table at those hearings, we faced two banks of seats for committee members curving in a semicircle that seemed to surround us. The seats were filled with unfamiliar and disbelieving faces. Behind us the open sections of the hearing room were filled to overflowing. There could be no mistake of the political power that had turned out to hear our testimony. But when we explained our decision, it was received with satisfaction, and the issue disappeared as quickly as it had arisen.

Gradually we worked our way through all these questions, and both EPA and the Corps built up a staff to run the program. At the outset, on December 23, 1970, only a handful of individuals at headquarters was assigned to the permit program. During the spring a small permit team was formed in each of our regional offices. OMB and Congress approved a supplemental budget authorizing 400 additional EPA members and 200 more Corps people for handling the workload. The hiring begun in anticipation of that approval continued, though most of the new employees had little experience in industrial waste control and no idea of the intricacies of the permit program they would be running.

The task of building the new recruits into an effective agency team fell chiefly to Bert Printz. He was only in his mid-thirties, but he proved a lucky choice. Printz had spent most of his professional life in the federal water pollution control program and had worked in both headquarters and regional offices. He had a talent for program development — and a glib tongue and a bouncy sense of humor. Bert was enough of a salesman and promoter to handle smoothly the never-ending criticism the program provoked. Most of his effort, however, went into building the staff, setting up a communications system of memos and bulletins to keep everyone up-to-date on all new details, and giving guidance on all those issues. He reported directly to me. We met together several times a week and often talked on the telephone. We were both up to our necks in the problems of this program, but there was a major difference. As an Assistant Administrator of EPA I had several other responsibilities and spent most of my time dealing with our outside critics. Printz spent all his time on this one program, and it was his job to make sure the work got done. In virtually every complicated program there is one person well below the Administrator who is the front man for all the agency's programs, responsible for the management of that specific program. In the case of the permit program, that person was Bert Printz, and our success — or failure — was largely in his hands.

July 1, 1971, was the deadline set by the President for every company to file its permit applications. Our original estimate was that forty thousand plants would require permits. In a slow trickle during June the application forms began to arrive, but by July 1 only three thousand applications — not forty thousand — had been filed. Suddenly the permit program was facing another unexpected crisis. The evidence that companies were not submitting their applications raised widespread doubts about the effectiveness of the program. Questions began to appear in the general press. In its "Periscope" section, *Newsweek* suggested that the federal permit program was collapsing. A similar item showed up on the front page of the *Wall Street Journal*.

By the end of the summer we knew we were caught in a struggle for survival. I had been in charge of the program by then for several months, and despite my original reservations I had become committed to its success. I was convinced that if we could overcome the early problems, the permit system would be a great step forward for pollution control. And because the program had emerged as one of the most publicized undertakings of EPA, its failure would undermine respect for the entire agency. It was obvious, though, that the rapid erosion of public support for the program was creating the risk of disaster. Legislation was starting through Congress to overhaul the Federal Water Pollution Control Act. Our immediate task was to preserve enough support for the program so that Congress would endorse it and keep it going under the new law.

As a first step we had to demonstrate that we could compel industry to submit the application forms. It was one of those critical times when people were judging the performance of a program, and public impressions would determine the future. We had to take some bold action to counteract the notion that the program was a fizzle. I decided to concentrate all our efforts on a campaign to bring law suits against companies that had failed to file. We hoped to collect a large number of cases and announce them all at once; that would maximize the public impact of our enforcement effort.

During the next several weeks EPA personnel scurried around the country, checking whether companies had filed their applications and collecting evidence to submit to U.S. Attorneys for prosecution. At this point, we encountered a surprise. We discovered that most of the big industrial plants had already filed. In other cases, an application seemed to appear a few days after the EPA inspectors visited a plant. The flow of applications was steadily swelling.

Many difficulties hampered our effort to collect an impressive group of enforcement cases. By mid-September we had thirty-five. They were not as many as I felt we needed, but it looked as if that was as many as I was going to get, and I decided to go ahead with a press conference to announce them. Once again I found that the press greeted our news skeptically. One reporter asked why we were bringing suit against only thirty-five plants. Another ridiculed the small fine, $2500, that could be levied under the Refuse Act and asked why we had not brought several counts against each plant (based on successive days of violation) to build up the fines. Several reporters wondered why so many of the plants were small ones, and I was embarrassed to discover, in the course of the press conference, that one of the plants was a saw mill on an Indian reservation. Why, a reported asked, were we going after the Indians rather than the large corporate polluters?

Despite all these weaknesses, there was enough in the package to convey the message that EPA was serious about enforcing compliance. I was able to make the point that we had carried out a full-scale national survey and were satisfied that nearly all of the two thousand to three thousand largest dischargers in the country had filed their applications. One factor gave the story some additional punch. Officials in U.S.

Steel apparently had resolved to contest the legality of the permit program by submitting unsigned applications. We placed three U.S. Steel plants among our cases referred for prosecution and said we would bring suit unless U.S. Steel substituted signed application forms. Within a few days U.S. Steel capitulated, agreeing to sign their applications, and we had made a significant breakthrough.

Completion of the enforcement drive to prosecute non-filers presaged the program's acceptance by the critics. We no longer were plagued by mention of the target of forty thousand applications that had been in the public mind for the previous nine months. Over fifteen thousand applications had been submitted, and they covered almost all of the large industrial polluters. We had also made it clear that the Environmental Protection Agency would act vigorously to carry out the program. Shortly afterward a favorable report written by Bert Schorr, one of the most respected writers in the environmental field, appeared in the *Wall Street Journal.* It pointed out that just the requirement to file a permit application was forcing industries to learn more about their waste discharges than they had ever known before. It also described several cases in which the program's requirements had already caused dischargers to clean up their pollution. Resistance by industry had been broken, and we began to receive growing public approval.

In November we received wonderful news. The Senate completed work on the new water pollution control legislation, and the bill gave us total support. It incorporated the permit program as a basic part of the new statutory framework. It also consolidated the federal effort entirely within EPA, eliminating the need to operate in an awkward joint venture with the Corps of Engineers. Suddenly our confidence was bolstered, and we felt that our work to get the program started would all be made worthwhile.

At the working level, however, where efforts had shifted

to processing the applications, a new problem came to the fore. It was one we had anticipated, but no one had dreamed of its severity. The review of individual application forms in our regional offices and by the district engineers revealed glaring inadequacies in the information submitted. In some forms many questions had not been answered at all. It turned out that almost every form required extensive work if we were to obtain information needed to write the pollution control requirements. We began our first efforts to develop those requirements and were slowly starting to make real progress, but yet another obstacle was about to block our path.

One weekday evening in early December I was at home with guests for dinner. The telephone rang. It was Stan Benjamin of the Associated Press: "What do you think of the *Kalur* decision?" "The what?" "Oh, maybe you haven't heard." That's right, I hadn't, but Stan told me all about it. A Federal District Court in Ohio had just handed down a devastating decision. The judge ruled that the permit program was subject to the requirements of the National Environmental Policy Act of 1969. We had believed that since the whole purpose of the program was to protect the environment, it was not subject to NEPA's requirements to write environmental impact statements. The judge disagreed. He issued an order that forbade the Corps of Engineers and EPA to issue any permits anywhere in the country until our regulations were revised to provide for environmental impact statements. Overwhelmed by the prospect of these additional burdens, which we knew we did not have the manpower to carry, we decided not to change our regulations, and we appealed the court order. We hoped that the Court of Appeals would reverse, but in the meantime issuance of permits was forbidden. With twenty-three thousand applications filed and twenty permits issued, the program stopped dead in its tracks.

The Senate bill and the *Kalur* decision largely eliminated the Corps of Engineers from the permit program. Faced with a court injunction, which had stopped the program for the time being, and the Senate bill, which excluded the Corps from the program in the future, the Corps had little incentive for working on permit activities. Within EPA, however, we viewed the *Kalur* decision as no more than a temporary setback. We assumed that somehow the problem would be cured, perhaps by pending legislation, and we had gone far enough in the permit-processing to know we had no time to lose in preparing draft permits so that we could be ready to function once the program started again. Indeed, the court order gave us time we badly needed to do our technical homework.

The *Kalur* decision in effect put the permit program into a cocoon for nearly an entire year. Controversy over the program died quickly as it all but disappeared from public sight. But for the staff of EPA these were months of intensive work. Permit applications were sorted out, and their data checked. On-site inspections were made at literally thousands of plants, and samples of the discharges were analyzed to determine existing pollution levels. This was slow work, and on the surface it was unproductive. But it was work that had to be done if our country was ever to achieve an effective pollution control program. We were gathering information on who was discharging what, establishing a data bank containing information on the sources of pollution.

All of this work built the foundation necessary to set the pollution control requirements, but on this point the agency confronted the problem I had predicted at CEQ. At a large meeting of regional staff personnel in January 1972, discussion concentrated on the perplexities of writing the cleanup requirements. Despite our work throughout the past year, we still had no formula for setting the pollution control requirements for all the different industrial plants. Jim

McDonald, director of our enforcement program in the Great Lakes region, stated the issue bluntly: "We really cannot even begin to write these permits until we make basic decisions on just how tough we're going to be." The point was obvious. The need indisputably clear. The answer nowhere in sight.

That problem involved perhaps the most fundamental question in the whole field of pollution control: How can you set requirements that are fair, that place equivalent demands on all plants despite the vast differences among them? EPA had already completed studies of fourteen major industries to try to develop guidelines for writing the permit requirements, but those studies had been inadequate. We needed to know what pollution would be produced by each type of industrial plant and what methods could be used to control it. Then we had to calculate the costs of control and work out requirements that would strike a fair balance among the varied industries. It was only as I listened to our regional staff express their frustrations that I began to appreciate fully how difficult and complicated that job was going to be. Under intense pressure, the best technical experts in the agency went to work to develop guidance that our staff could rely on in writing the permits.

During 1972, the morale of the people working on the permits began to suffer badly. The program was well into its second year, and we still had no positive results to show for our efforts. Major issues confronted us, and several of those issues could not really be resolved until the new law was enacted. If the final form of that law was different from what we hoped it would be, much of the work we were now doing might have to be done over. We were betting on the future, and the future might never come. Nevertheless, the efforts went forward.

While hundreds of EPA employees struggled to work out the permit requirements, we watched with anxiety the progress of the water pollution law as it made its way through Congress. The whole future of the program depended on that bill. My own special worry was whether we could obtain an exemption from the requirement imposed by the *Kalur* decision to write environmental impact statements on all our major permits. I had done everything I could think of to drum up support for Congress to include that exemption. Most environmentalists, however, were opposed to our being granted an exemption; they feared any precedent that might vitiate the impact statement law. A "Save NEPA" committee of environmentalists had rallied opposition against any changes, and our first efforts to obtain relief failed to evoke support.

Throughout the summer of 1972, the new water pollution law, like the permit program, was dormant. A conference committee was settling differences between the House and Senate bills, but the sessions were held behind closed doors, and we could not learn what decisions the committee was making. Week by week the time passed by. Then one morning in October the suspense ended. I received an unexpected telephone call from Jim Jordan, a legislative aide to Senator Howard Baker, who had worked closely with me on the issue of the exemption. He broke the news that the conference committee had finally completed its work and reported out a bill. And he added, with a triumphant ring in his voice, that on the previous day, at the very last of the thirty-nine conference committee sessions, he had interjected into the closing debate a provision to exempt the permit program from the environmental impact statement requirements. The provision had been adopted and would almost certainly be enacted. That was the news I wanted to hear.

October 17, 1972, was the day of decision. A climactic vote by the House of Representatives completed the enactment of the Federal Water Pollution Control Act Amendments of

1972. It happened to be the day of another large regional meeting on the permit program in Washington, and the news came in to me on a hand-written note. When I read the note aloud, the room burst with applause. It had been a long wait. Some in that room had worked full-time on the permit program for more than two years, overcoming one obstacle after another. During the past year our full-time staff for this program alone had grown to 350. We had held the twenty-three thousand permit applications in our files for over a year. Now we had the green light. It was full speed ahead.

Full speed ahead, however, did not mean that the job would be completed quickly. The new statute was eighty-nine single-spaced printed pages, and it presented a bewildering array of requirements. It took several months for us to read the statute, debate its ambiguities, and set a strategy for carrying out the program. The new law established a complicated arrangement to bring the state agencies actively into the permit program, and inevitably it required a new set of basic regulations. Our greatest challenge remained: we had to determine the costly cleanup requirements for thousands of industrial plants in the only way that they could be handled — one plant at a time. By the end of June 1973, the total number of all permits issued throughout the country was still fewer than 300.

At long last, however, the permit program was really ready to roll. A strong national organization had been built and its people trained in their assignments. The twenty-three thousand permit applications had been checked and their discharge data verified. Legal and policy issues had been resolved. Working relationships between EPA and state personnel were improving. The slow trickle of permits being issued swelled to a flow of several hundred a month. The statute indicated a deadline of the end of 1974 for the issuance of the permits, and people worked against that deadline to cover all of the major pollution problems. Even by December 1974 the whole job had not been completed, but by far the most onerous part of the task was over. EPA and state agencies had issued regulatory permits to over fourteen thousand industrial plants during the previous eighteen months. These included nearly all of the three thousand biggest industrial water pollution problems in the country.

The issuance of these permits marked a long step forward in our national effort to control water pollution. The most important improvement is that the permits establish detailed requirements that apply to individual plants. They impose deadlines to install pollution control equipment and set clear limits on the discharges that are permitted. These requirements are more sophisticated and precise controls than we have ever before had in the fight against water pollution.

The level of control required by these permits is more stringent than the requirements they replaced. Each plant, therefore, must normally undertake an extensive abatement program to reduce its discharges and submit regular reports on any pollution it is releasing. The 1972 law requires that these reports be made available for public inspection. In addition, the law imposes heavy penalties for permit violations, including fines of up to $25,000 per day.

Just as impressive to me as all these improvements is the time that was required to bring them about. The President's permit program was announced on December 23, 1970, and Congress confirmed the program in October 1972. Despite the intensive efforts that went into the program from its start, it was not until *four years later* that most of the permits were issued. Even then the job was by no means over. Thousands of small plants that discharge pollutants still did not have permits. In addition, many plants contested the permits that were issued. Under the regulations, any company had a right to appeal its permit, and this could mean a formal administrative hearing that might, in some cases, be followed by judicial review. Several hundred large industrial plants took advantage of this right, which usually delayed a start on their abatement programs. U.S. Steel, for example, challenged almost every permit issued to it, and by 1976 its lawyers were still fighting the requirements for most of its plants.

Above and beyond all the time needed to issue the permits, much more work must be done to clean up the pollution. To design and install equipment for a major abatement program usually requires a full three years. So if EPA or a state issued a permit in 1974 and the company accepted its terms, it normally would not be until 1977 that the real benefits of that permit would show up as cleaner water in the river.

The public is often impatient for government programs to produce results. The debate over national problems may foster the illusion that the government ought to be able to make immediate progress. Nothing shatters that illusion more rapidly than a careful look at what is actually required to put a complicated program into operation. The lag-time is measured in years, not in weeks or months.

The time required to carry out a program does not begin, however, until there is a policy decision to start the effort. What the public almost never understands is how long it takes to make such basic policy decisions after the emergence of a problem that requires government action. In fact, the delays in getting started in solving national problems are likely to dwarf the delays in implementing government programs. In the case of pollution, decades of abuse preceded any efforts at control, even after the damage was obvious. The reasons for this slow response are embedded in the system that controls basic government policy. The key to understanding this system is first to recognize its bewildering complexity. The place to begin is the tangled web of relationships within the bureaucracy of any agency and among it, the White House, and the Congress.

CHAPTER 7

EPA and the White House

THE DAY AFTER Nixon won the 1972 election, Cabinet officers and agency heads were summoned to a White House meeting. Gathered together in the flush of triumph that an election victory creates, these men were in for a jolt. They all were asked to submit their resignations so that the President could decide whether he wanted to keep them in their positions. They were also told to obtain letters of resignation from their sub-Cabinet officers. That started a period of several weeks in which the highest officials in the Nixon Administration, men who had worked for the President for several years, wondered whether they were about to be summarily canned. In several cases the Cabinet officers were reappointed, but some of their subordinates were reshuffled.

It was nearly Christmas before Ruckelshaus received any word about his future. He was called out of a meeting at the White House to be shown a press release announcing his reappointment. Inwardly burning at this high-handed treatment, Ruckelshaus stunned the Nixon press officer by responding that no one had talked to him about the reappointment and that under the current conditions he was not at all sure that he wanted to continue. Caught by surprise, White House aides hurriedly arranged for Ruckelshaus to meet with President Nixon.

In his meeting with the President, Ruckelshaus stipulated the two conditions under which he would continue to serve.

One was that his top staff would not be changed. The other was that the system previously established for clearance of EPA regulations by the President's Office of Management and Budget must be clarified so that final authority over regulatory decisions clearly rested within EPA. President Nixon agreed to both of these conditions, and Ruckelshaus returned to EPA exultant. He announced to the press that, having received sufficient assurances of EPA's independence, he would remain as Administrator.

Receiving those assurances in conversation with President Nixon was one thing; making them stick was quite another. Below the President were tiers of staff in the White House, OMB, and the other federal departments. The men on these staffs had their own ideas of how things should run, and their desires were fortified by established practice. The existing system had been set up by OMB Director George Schultz as a result of the controversy caused by EPA's first set of major regulations under the 1970 Clean Air Act. It was a procedure of interagency review, which gave other departments a chance to criticize all EPA regulations before they could be issued. The new system created uncertainty over whether EPA or OMB was really in control of the major decisions concerning the content of our regulations. This was the subject of Senator Eagleton's oversight hearings in February 1972, and it was a topic of controversy long after those hearings had ended.

After the interagency review system was established in 1971, all new regulations underwent an extensive review managed directly by the OMB staff, and many were delayed for months when other departments disagreed with the regulations. The new system forced EPA to perform far more thorough analyses of cost and other factors, but it also created opportunities for delay and red tape. The move from the extreme of independent action to the extreme of requiring what amounted to a consensus made clear to us the need for a better balance. EPA had to reclaim control over the development of its regulations, and President Nixon had promised it could do so. Despite that promise, we bargained in vain with OMB to spell out the change in writing.

It was not until after Ruckelshaus had left EPA to become Acting Director of the FBI and Russell Train was appointed Administrator of EPA in the summer of 1973 that EPA obtained written confirmation that the Administrator held ultimate authority over the content of EPA regulations. Train quietly but firmly insisted that this was the prerequisite for his being able to function effectively. Even then there remained the necessity to test the agreement in practice, and one of the critical tests occurred in December of 1973. At issue were regulations designed to protect public health by limiting amounts of lead in gasoline. The background was both involved and controversial.

When Congress wrote the Clean Air Act in 1970, it recognized that controlling auto pollution might involve the use of a new device called a "catalyst," which could convert the polluting hydrocarbons and carbon monoxide into harmless carbon dioxide and water. Since the effectiveness of catalysts could be destroyed if they were exposed to even small amounts of lead, the act authorized the EPA Administrator to prohibit or limit the amount of lead in gasoline. In addition, the act also directed EPA to examine the effects on health of the use of lead and other gasoline additives, and authorized the Administrator to control the use of any additives if he found they might endanger public health. The act thus provided two separate grounds for regulating the composition of gasoline.

The purpose of adding lead to gasoline is to increase its octane rating and to prevent its causing a "knock" in the engine. By 1973, refineries were putting well over 200,000 tons of lead a year into the national supply of gasoline. The processors of this lead had a huge financial stake in its continued usage. Most important of these was the Ethyl Corporation, a giant company with headquarters in Richmond, Virginia, close to the centers of political power in Washington.

For years the use of lead as a gasoline additive had been attacked by some scientists as a threat to public health. The horrors of lead poisoning have long been apparent, especially in the several thousand infants in cities each year who suffer brain damage from excessive levels of lead in their blood. At first this tragedy was attributed entirely to the infants' swallowing lead-based paint peeling from the walls in old houses. Beyond this obvious association of cause and effect, however, most aspects of the exposure of humans to lead and its effect on their health have remained subject to intense scientific debate.

It is clear that human beings in our country today are exposed to lead from several sources and that many people, especially children, absorb lead into their bodies in amounts that cause adverse effects on their health. Their exposure is most easily measured by the levels of lead in their blood. If the levels of lead are high, people may suffer kidney damage, irreversible neurological impairment, mental retardation, and death. They may show such symptoms of lead poisoning as anemia, severe intestinal cramps, and irritability.

A number of additional adverse health effects have been found in children exposed to lower lead concentrations, in the range described as "undue lead absorption." These effects may include minimal brain damage and behavioral disorders. They can impair a child's ability to concentrate or to discriminate between shapes and spatial relationships. They can interfere with a child's physical coordination and reaction time, such as his or her eye-hand coordination. Some surveys conducted in cities indicated that approximately 25 percent of the children tested showed undue lead absorption.

The other side of the Statue of Liberty

The old swimming hole, 1970s-style: this Lake Erie beach near Cleveland was closed because of pollution. Some of the beaches near Cleveland have recently been reopened, however, reflecting progress in pollution control.

Opposite, above: Dead fish and debris clog the Hudson River below Albany, New York, in 1970. Such episodes led to the enactment of the Federal Water Pollution Control Act of 1972.

Below: A real-estate corporation built these artificial reefs at Marco Island in Florida. But in April, 1976, the U.S. Army Corps of Engineers denied the company permission to develop the remaining natural areas of the islands.

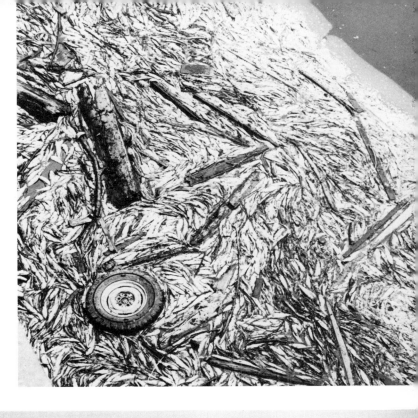

Rush-hour traffic congests the Southeast Freeway in Houston, one of the 38 cities cited for excessive auto pollution under the Clean Air Act.

As court cases drag on, the Reserve Mining plant at Silver Bay,
Minnesota, continues to discharge 67,000 tons of waste per day into
Lake Superior.

Walter J. Hickel, the first
Secretary of the Interior in
the Nixon administration, with
a young fisherman.

The first EPA administrator,
William Ruckelshaus, announces
the auto emission decision
in 1973.

Ruckelshaus (left) stands with
his successor, Russell Train
(center), and the author
at Train's swearing-in.

A dangerously persistent smog hangs over Birmingham in November, 1971. The EPA obtained a court order against 23 firms, all of which, including the U.S. Steel plant (below), were required to shut down. It was the first such action under the emergency powers of the Clean Air Act.

These two photos show the Florida Power and Light plant at Turkey Point, Florida, before and after the government compelled it to build a system of dikes and canals five miles long. These cool and recycle the hot water that otherwise would kill offshore marine life.

Above, young Arkansans clear up litter, while Stanley P. Spisiak, a Buffalo businessman who has become the area's unofficial environmental watchdog, investigates the effects of illegal oil dumping on the Buffalo River. In the late 1960s, the river caught fire three times in one two-year period.

Not even the wide-open spaces of the West are immune to pollution.
A pastoral mountain valley in Colorado contrasts with an Inferno-like
scene in Arizona—the culprit being a copper smelter dimly glimpsed
amid the haze, top center.

Two lakes near Dallas make another vivid contrast.

Human exposure to lead may come from the food we eat, the water we drink, the air we breathe, the dust in our homes, or, in the case of children, from peelings of leaded paint that have been ingested. It is the total body burden of lead absorbed from all these sources that will determine the severity of the effects of lead poisoning. The lead processors vigorously disagreed that airborne lead contributed at all to human health problems, but a great deal of evidence suggested the contrary. Studies have shown that people exposed to auto exhaust in their occupations, such as parking attendants or garage mechanics, frequently suffered excessive lead absorption. Other studies have shown a correlation between high levels of lead in the air and high blood lead levels in inner-city populations as compared to lower levels of airborne lead and blood lead levels in the suburbs of those cities.

In the case of children, however, the biggest threat from airborne lead may occur after it settles and contaminates the dust where they may be playing. Extremely high lead concentrations have been found in the street dust of large cities, and lead-containing dust has also been found on the hands of inner-city children and on floors and windowsills inside their homes. In Rochester, average blood lead levels among three- and four-year-old urban children were approximately double those found among suburban children. And in Newark, investigators found that the frequency of excessive lead absorption among children living within 100 feet of a heavily traveled roadway was twice that found among children living more than 100 or 200 feet away.

From these and other studies the best scientific experts in EPA had concluded that the incidence of excessive lead absorption among city children was a major health problem and that lead-contaminated dust was contributing significantly to that problem. Since the 200,000 tons a year of lead from gasoline blown out in auto exhaust accounted for roughly 90 percent of airborne lead, that was clearly one place to attack the problem.

In February 1972, EPA climaxed months of work on the subject of lead in gas by publishing two proposed regulations requiring reductions in the use of lead. One was based on the expectation that the auto makers would install catalysts on 1975 cars to meet the stricter pollution control standards that would come into effect that year. It required the oil industry to make one grade of lead-free gasoline, suitable for the 1975 cars, which would be generally available to all large gasoline stations around the country. This would cut out lead additives entirely for the new cars equipped with catalysts, but they would be only a small fraction of the total number of cars on the highway. The other proposed regulation was based directly on health considerations. It required that the lead content in all grades of gasoline be reduced by half over a four-year period. Because these "low-lead" regulations would apply to all gasoline, they called for a greater overall reduction. In the weeks allowed for public comment, both regulations received heavy criticism, but opposition from the oil industry, and especially from the manufacturers of lead additives, focused on the health-based regulations. Industry argued that available scientific data did not prove that adverse health effects result from lead in gasoline. After intense backstage argument, EPA dropped its plans to bring out the two regulations simultaneously. In January 1973, it promulgated the requirements for lead-free gasoline to be available for use in catalyst-equipped cars, and it proposed again the low-lead regulations, with a revised explanation of the adverse health effects, emphasizing the threat from lead-contaminated dust.

That action did nothing to quell the debate over the health-based regulations. The oil companies and lead processors continued to tell their side of the story, and environmentalists complained that EPA had ducked the real issue.

Senator Hart of Michigan, who chaired the congressional hearings on the issue, exhorted EPA to eliminate lead from all gasoline. With the scientific debate over the health questions and the intense pulling and hauling from both directions, EPA might easily have postponed action indefinitely. What brought matters to a head was a law suit by the Natural Resources Defense Council in which a federal judge ordered the Administrator to produce the health regulations not later than December 3, 1973. That court order pushed the subject to the top of the priority list, and wheels began to grind within the agency. EPA distributed its draft regulations to the other agencies in mid-November. We requested written comments within one week. Timing would be tight to meet the court deadline, and the complexity of the issues added to the uncertainty of our meeting it.

Though I had not been involved in development of these regulations, it was my lot to shepherd them through the final stages of the interagency review. Ten days before the court deadline, I called John Sawhill at OMB and asked for a prompt meeting to thrash out the comments from the other agencies. I knew we would have to go through the interagency review before putting out the regulations, and I had to get the process started quickly.

John Sawhill was then an Assistant Director of OMB. His job, though nearly hidden from public view, had immense importance. He was responsible for the budget and many policy decisions for all the federal programs affecting the environment, natural resources, and several other fields. That put him smack into the pressure cooker, and the demands of his job required an intense night-and-day dedication. During my five years with the government, Sawhill was the fifth man to hold that job. He had held the post only a few months, and was destined to stay there only a few months longer before bouncing up and into even greater controversy as head of the Federal Energy Administration.

There his aggressive advocacy of energy conservation and his conflicts with other powerful figures would bring about his resignation, but in November of 1973 such a fiery future seemed far from likely for John Sawhill. Behind his heavy horn-rimmed glasses, he seemed mild, even studious. He had been trained as an economist and had come to OMB from a promising business career in management and financial analysis. Still in his late thirties, Sawhill had little experience in the exercise of political power. Yet in his position at OMB he had strategic power over EPA and was one of the chief figures we had to deal with in the whole White House structure.

We regarded John Sawhill as a pretty good draw for the job. He had been friendly and fair in my several contacts with him; he did not throw his weight around, and I felt I could trust what he said. He also seemed to have a true feeling for environmental concerns, though I knew that his job required him to put aside personal inclinations. As chief arbiter of interagency disputes his role would be to act more as a referee than as the judge in the conflicting arguments.

In response to my request, Sawhill scheduled a meeting for the Friday after Thanksgiving, and on the afternoon of Thanksgiving Day I excused myself from family and in-laws to retreat to the basement, where a laundry table formed a desk, and began to pore over the lengthy briefing documents. In thirty fact-crammed pages Dave Hanson, a bright, hard-working young analyst, had put together the whole background of the subject and the debates on the key issues. I tried to soak up as much knowledge as I could to prepare for the arguments that would be coming my way the next afternoon.

I spent much of Friday morning in further study of the written materials and in discussions of the issues with the EPA staff. At the start of the afternoon a small group of us went over to HEW to discuss the health issues. We then proceeded to the Executive Office Building for the meeting Sawhill had scheduled. This was the apex of the usual interagency review process. The regulations had already been analyzed by staff in each agency, and normally any disputes would be argued out at a lower level. In this case a "meeting of principals" was needed because of the court deadline and because the lead-in-gas regulations were obviously going to raise major disputes.

We checked in at the guard's desk of the EOB, that old, hulking, ornate building at the corner of 17th Street and Pennsylvania Avenue, and presented our identification cards for approval by guards impressively dressed in white gold-trimmed uniforms. Then we walked up two flights of the wide curved stairway and went into Room 248. It was a familiar arena. A large oval conference table with seats for sixteen people filled almost all of the room. Additional chairs lined the walls. With its high ceiling, rich molding, and handsome chandeliers, the room might once have provided an elegant setting, but its design had been marred to provide for piping and air conditioning, and its color scheme — drab tan walls and light green vinyl chairs — set the tone of a no-frills workshop that accorded with the usual functions of the room. We moved down along the table to take seats toward one end, at a slight angle across from the center chair, where John Sawhill would sit.

Top officers were present from HEW, the National Science Foundation, the Interior Department, the Department of Commerce, OMB, and the White House Office of Energy Policy. Looking around the room, I saw several strange faces and a few people I knew well from many previous sessions. A few seats to my right was Ray Peck, the ever-contentious advocate from the Department of Commerce; I knew what his approach would be. Next to him was Steve Wakefield, Assistant Secretary of the Department of the Interior. I guessed that he would protest the impact of our regulations

on oil supply. Before joining Interior he had practiced law
with one of the biggest firms in Texas, but I had no idea what
his personal beliefs might be. In our few contacts he had
seemed thoughtful and moderate — more a lawyer than a
Texan, I thought. To my left, toward the other end of the
table, were representatives from the other health agencies,
including HEW, which had previously questioned our health
effects studies. I wondered what position they would take at
this meeting. One person who was not present was Dick
Fairbanks. Fairbanks, once a Special Assistant to
Ruckelshaus at EPA, had left him to work for John Whitaker
on the White House Domestic Council, and later had succeeded Whitaker as the chief member of the White House
staff active in our area. Because of his position, Fairbanks
might have been expected to weigh in on this issue. Bright,
tough, and fiercely ambitious, Dick Fairbanks could be a
potent force to deal with, and I wondered whether his
absence meant he would not get involved in this problem.

When the meeting got underway, we discussed the health
issues, briefly, but our attention was focused on the adverse
effects the regulations might have on the supply of oil. We
knew that taking lead out of gasoline could mean that more
oil would be needed to produce the same amount of gasoline.
The Arab embargo had been imposed just the previous
month, and with each passing week the threat of critical
shortages of oil had grown more severe. Steve Wakefield
argued that Interior's figures differed from those of EPA on
the effect that removal of lead would have on crude-oil
consumption. He said that our regulations would cause a loss
of 1 percent of the national supply of crude oil. Ray Peck
argued that the loss would be even greater. We batted the
arguments back and forth.

As usual in these interagency meetings around the large
conference table at OMB, nobody defended the proposed
EPA regulations other than EPA. Opinions from all the

others ranged from hostility to neutrality. Nevertheless, I felt that the intensity of opposition was not remarkably high, and I heard no persuasive argument against our regulations. I mentioned to John Sawhill as the meeting ended that we would put out the regulations the next Wednesday, and explained that even if we accepted Interior's prediction of a 1 percent crude-oil penalty, that would not outweigh considerations of health. It was evident that we had not yet cleared away all objections, but the prospects for moving ahead seemed more encouraging at the end of the day than I could possibly have hoped in the morning. We walked out of the building into the darkness and relative quiet of the street hushed by the holiday weekend, and I went home for two days' rest.

During the morning on Monday I received a message that Interior's two experts on the oil industry could meet with me that afternoon. A great deal of work remained to be done by Wednesday, however, and I checked with several members of the EPA staff to see if they could move it along. The job of preparing the final form of the regulations and preamble was not yet begun, but the EPA's Public Affairs Office was preparing a press release and other materials for the announcement.

Toward the latter part of the morning a tiny cloud appeared on the horizon. I learned that Sawhill's office had scheduled a meeting for six o'clock that evening for Dick Fairbanks and me to discuss the regulations. In our discussions Friday, John and I had delicately skirted around the underlying question of the interagency review — whether EPA was free to proceed with the regulations without obtaining OMB approval. My position, implicit but not spelled out in my comments, was that we had gone through the interagency review, had heard all the arguments, and had made our decision to go forward. I had made that clear to Sawhill. Yet I also knew that John assumed we would not proceed if major disagreements remained unsolved. Normally the two approaches could be accommodated, because there would be time to reach agreement on a decision that the agency could support and others could accept. But normality was pushed askew by the time schedule we were following, and I felt myself moving on a collision course.

Our regulations and press materials were already being typed. If sharp disagreement developed at the six o'clock meeting, there would be little time left to resolve any questions. I called Sawhill to get some feel for his thinking but could not reach him, so I called Fairbanks. It was immediately clear that we were in for a rough time. Dick came on strong. He said he was under strict orders that he had no authority to approve the release of the regulations (thereby staking out his claim that we could not proceed without his approval) and that Mel Laird had said that "those regulations would go out over his dead body."

This came as a jolt. It was the first suggestion from anyone that Laird had any interest in these regulations, but obviously he would be a force to reckon with. After a prominent career in Congress, Laird had served as President Nixon's first Secretary of Defense. He then retired from the government but had returned a short while later during the Watergate crisis to become a counselor to the President, with immense responsibilities across the range of domestic affairs. He was at that time one of the two or three most powerful men in the Nixon White House.

Now the picture was really clouded. I had never laid eyes on Mel Laird and had no idea how he would approach this issue. Nor had I any idea whether Laird was deeply interested in this problem or whether Fairbanks was simply playing a high card to shake us. What I did know was that we were only forty-eight hours away from the court-ordered deadline, and that big objections meant big trouble. I pointed out to Fairbanks that we were far advanced in our planning of the regulations, that we had had no knowledge of his position, and that I felt strongly that our regulations were proper. Then I asked what his objections were. We discussed the regulations at length but made little progress, and finally agreed that we would have to pick up our discussion at the meeting later that day.

At one o'clock the Interior experts came into my office. Munching a cold cheeseburger from the Roy Rogers snack bar on the ground floor, I waved them to a seat. I knew these two men could be crucial to the whole puzzle. If their objections could be satisfied, that would be the key to neutralizing Wakefield, which in turn might be the key to pacifying Sawhill and Fairbanks. Their major concern was that our requirements for the first year (1975) of the phasedown would have a disruptive effect on the industry. The more I listened, the more persuasive their arguments appeared. Later that afternoon, I asked the EPA staff to reexamine the first-year requirements. As we argued out the issue among ourselves, we began to see that we could eliminate Interior's most serious objections by easing the first-year requirements, without changing the more stringent requirements for the second, third, and fourth years. In view of the emergency problems facing the petroleum industry for 1974 and 1975, this seemed to make sense.

At six o'clock I appeared in Sawhill's office and began the meeting with him, Fairbanks, and a member of each man's staff. Sawhill's desk was a large, completely round table in one corner of his spacious office, which looked out over the headlights of traffic moving slowly on 17th Street. I sat on one side, and the four of them sat opposite me. I had the feeling that this was the real showdown. No other federal agency was represented, but this was the culmination of the interagency review. Earlier confrontations enabled critical issues to surface, so that Cabinet officers could appeal directly to the top or, as in this case, so that White House staff could intervene and pursue the argument. I knew that if we could settle the issues at this meeting, Sawhill and Fairbanks could commit the White House and we would have no further questions from Mel Laird or others, but if we ended in disagreement, we might have to carry the dispute to a higher level. The meeting also showed the power of the White House staff — it was only because of Dick Fairbanks that we were still receiving flak about our regulations. I thought to myself that if he had been sick, out of town, uninformed, or in agreement we would not have had this trouble.

Fairbanks opened the meeting by proposing a "compromise," under which EPA would announce that lead in gasoline did cause some health problems but that no further regulations were required because the quantities of lead in gasoline would be reduced sufficiently as the lead-free (catalyst) regulations took effect. I answered that those regulations would not reduce lead use fast enough; in addition, if catalysts should be abandoned, the regulations would lose their effect. We then probed every angle. For an hour and a quarter they blasted away at me and I fired back at them.

Sitting in one corner of John Sawhill's spacious office that afternoon, far removed from the public eye, the five of us acted out in microcosm the drama of the entire environmental debate. The others challenged EPA's health data. Some scientists believed airborne lead was no problem, they said. How could we justify government interference, imposing burdensome regulations and costs on industry, when we could not prove that lead in gasoline definitely caused health damage? It was impossible for me to present an ironclad defense. I was no scientist and no expert in this issue, but I had studied it thoroughly and I tried to apply my common sense. I knew that lead poisoning was a widespread health problem, damaging human lives, especially children's. I knew that lead in gasoline was the predominant source of airborne lead and one of the major sources of all lead entering the environment. I knew that many scientists, including our experts at EPA, were convinced that lead in gasoline was contributing directly to the detrimental health effects. I knew that lead could be removed from gasoline at a cost that would not be disruptive. Still, I could not prove that this change had to be made.

It was the age-old dilemma. Is pollution always to be permitted until its damage can be proven beyond any doubt? Outnumbered four to one in the argument, I was on the defensive in justifying EPA's regulations. But that was the point. The law placed the responsibility for this decision in EPA, and for the purposes of that argument I was the EPA. I knew that lead had been in gasoline since I myself was a child. I thought of the thousands of children who might have been — probably had been — severely damaged by its subtle, poisoning effects. And I was damned if I was going to be bulldozed because I didn't have answers for every one of Dick Fairbanks's questions. We finally broke up the meeting with no resolution. Driving home at the end of a long day, I felt the problems looming larger and larger.

As I was finishing dinner that evening, I received a telephone call from Russ Train. We discussed the regulations over the telephone for an hour and a half, going over every issue. We agreed that he would get in touch with Sawhill to emphasize his belief that we should issue the regulations, and as we hung up he said he would call John, even though it was 10:15, because he (Train) was leaving the next morning on a seven o'clock plane for Kansas City. A half-hour later he called back to report that he had talked at length with Sawhill and thought he had helped to convince him of the merits of our position.

By the next morning we were fast approaching the point of no return. In our long discussion the night before, Russ and I had agreed to modify the requirements for 1975 to ease the first-year impact on the petroleum industry. I promptly called two technical experts at Interior and Steve Wakefield to inform them of our decision. Their delight at that change indicated to me that their chief objections had now been satisfied. I also called Sawhill and then Fairbanks to tell them the news.

A meeting of the Domestic Council's Committee on the Environment was scheduled for three-thirty that afternoon, and I knew that I would see Sawhill, Fairbanks, Wakefield, and others at the meeting. By the time I left EPA to attend that session in the White House, it was time for the Public Affairs Office to announce the press conference. This would be the point from which there could be no turning back, except at the price of profound embarrassment. Arriving at the White House, I learned that the three-thirty meeting would be delayed. An urgent session on energy was still running in the Roosevelt Room. I pulled Dick Fairbanks from the midst of the crowd of people waiting for the meeting to begin and asked if he had had a chance to explore our regulations further with the people at Interior. He responded by suggesting that he and I sit down with Sawhill and Wakefield after the meeting ended. I agreed to this, but I pointed out that it was getting too late for us to make any changes in our documents. To meet the court deadline we would be holding a press conference at 3:00 P.M. the next day, at which we would make known the regulations. When Fairbanks made no protest over the plans for the press conference, I picked up a White House telephone and called back to my office to instruct that the conference be announced.

By the time the meeting ended it was half-past five, and for convenience the four of us decided to stay in the Roosevelt Room to discuss the lead-in-gas regulations. It was a large, comfortably furnished room in the center of the main floor of the West Wing, with a long conference table running down the center of the room and a sofa and easy chairs off to the sides. We took the chairs at one end of the table and started right in where we had left off the night before, though with one vital improvement. Fairbanks and Sawhill both recognized that EPA was going to issue health-based regulations. The basic question of whether the health effects from lead in gas warranted regulation was no longer in controversy, and the area of dispute was narrowed down to what the regulations should be.

Fairbanks offered a new compromise. He said that Interior was satisfied with our requirements for the first year, as modified that day, since they would entail little or no burden on the industry in addition to the lead-free regulations. He then proposed that we relax our requirements for each of the subsequent years so that they would duplicate the effect of the regulations we had previously issued to require lead-free gas be provided for the catalyst-equipped cars that would be coming on to the market after 1975. I said no, and with rising emotions we argued back and forth. I felt the modifications we had already made answered the objections sufficiently, and I was determined not to make further concessions just because of their opposition. Anger rose in Fairbanks's voice. The tension snapped on an unrelated point.

The night before, Russ Train had sent congressional leaders a proposal to modify the statutory automobile emission standards for nitrogen oxides. There had been disagreement over what type of modification to propose, and Fairbanks and others had been working with EPA for a couple of months to develop an administration position. On a sudden request from Congress, EPA had sent the package up without obtaining the customary approval from the White House. When John Sawhill mentioned this, Fairbanks exploded. He stood up, shouted, "What's the use of holding meetings?" slammed his pencil down on the table, and stomped out of the room. A few moments later, John Sawhill followed, and some ten minutes after that, as I sat in stony silence, I was informed that they were discussing the matter with Mel Laird. After twenty or thirty minutes, Fairbanks and Sawhill marched back into the room. They said that it was obvious we were getting nowhere in attempting to settle the question and that it would have to be discussed at a higher level by Train and Laird. They explained that Laird had tried to reach Russ by telephone and had not yet succeeded but hoped to reach him soon.

Seeing no point in my remaining, I picked up my briefcase and started to leave the room. As I approached the door Dick Fairbanks was again complaining about EPA's having sent the nitrogen oxides package to the Hill without obtaining clearance by the White House. "No wonder people say they can't trust EPA," he said. By then I was only a few feet away. I glared at him and shot back, "Let me tell you about that package." My mind was flooded with the tensions and harassments attendant on trying to meet deadlines, to respond to congressional requests, to push ahead toward dozens of different program objectives, to thrash out an endless series of policy issues and try to reach agreement with the countless different faces who took exception, and, above all, to communicate, to communicate, to communicate. Russ Train had tried to call John Sawhill three times the previous day to discuss that proposal with him before signing the letters and sending them up, but he had not been able to reach him. Fairbanks was glaring back at me. "Yeah, why don't you tell me about that nitrogen oxides package," he said sarcastically. Our glances locked in one of those fleeting instants that is captured and stored in the memory, the intense seeds of momentary hatred sprouting behind the exterior of a cold blank face. "No, I don't think I will," I said, and, turning away in disgust, I walked out of the room and out of the White House and into the welcome chill of the evening darkness.

In the game of cajolery, bluff, and honest argument that formed the final phase of determining the lead-in-gas regulations, the Lady of Fortune had dealt us a lucky card. It was the fact that Mel Laird had been unable to reach Russ Train. If he had, there would have been a significant and perhaps decisive difference in the outcome. Caught before hearing of the arguments I had been through, Russ would have been at a hopeless disadvantage not knowing what points he should cover and what arguments he should make. Laird, on the other hand, relying on information from Fairbanks and Sawhill and without a presentation of EPA's side, would have drawn conclusions against us. There was no doubt as to my next step. It was one time I was grateful I had a telephone in my car. Before the car was out of the driveway, I had the telephone at my ear and was dialing our office trying to reach Russ Train before Mel Laird did. I reached Russ's executive assistant, Roger Strelow, who had just received the call from the White House and was attempting to reach Russ. We quickly agreed that he would postpone calling Russ until I got back to the office and could brief him on what had happened.

For the rest of the ride back I sat still in the darkness. We drove around the Tidal Basin and past the Jefferson Memorial, quiet and lovely, lit up against the night. Inside, however, I was fuming. Almost never had I felt so bitterly angry. We had gone through the procedures agreed to long before. I had heard all the arguments from the other side, and they were unpersuasive. The decision should be ours to make. If there was a sound reason against what we proposed, we could take that into account — we were not inflexible — but there was none. And the objections that were raised came too late. The time for registering protest was last Friday. Where had Fairbanks been then? Could he not see the problems of raising basic objections so late in the game?

When I got back to the office it was seven-thirty. We

caught Russ just as he was arriving at the EPA laboratory in Kansas City. A large group of employees had remained two hours after closing time to be at the laboratory during the Administrator's first visit, but Russ took our telephone call before beginning his tour. I announced that things had gone from bad to worse and gave a complete run-down of what had happened. He agreed to call Laird, and I left the office to drive home.

As I got out of the car my daughter Nancy welcomed me by shouting that Mr. Train was on the phone. He had just ended a long telephone conversation with Mel Laird and felt enormously relieved. He said that Laird definitely had an open mind on the regulations but had wanted the various agencies to work out their disagreements. Laird had understood that HEW opposed our regulations, but Russ told him that HEW was neutral. Laird had understood that Interior had great objections to our regulations, but Russ explained that their major objections had been satisfied. Russ had pointed out that we were under a court order to issue regulations and that he would be subject to contempt if he did not issue them the next day. Laird had not known of this at all. Russ had also described in detail the circumstances under which he had sent the nitrogen oxides package to the Hill and his efforts to reach Sawhill first. Finally, Russ had asked Laird what his position was on the regulations, and Laird had answered that he really had no position. He said he did not know enough about the issues to have a position; he had hoped we could work one out through OMB. We had, to put it in the kindest terms possible, cast doubt on Fairbanks's statement of the previous day, his declaration that Laird had said the regulations would go out "over his dead body."

By the time Russ finished his explanation he had been at the regional laboratory for nearly an hour and a half — all on the telephone. It was time for him to leave and he had not yet begun the tour. It was clear, however, that one other step had to be taken, namely, to call Sawhill. We both agreed that Russ should make the call, and I slipped a TV dinner into the oven and poured myself a drink of Scotch. A little before eleven the telephone rang; Russ was calling from his hotel room, the Harry Truman Suite at the Muehlebach Hotel. He had had a good discussion with Sawhill. He felt that Sawhill was generally in agreement that we should proceed to issue the regulations, though he wanted to consider further the numerical standards. We agreed that I would put the regulations in final form and proceed with the press conference. Wearily I tumbled into bed.

It was still dark when I awoke, my mind and my stomach both churning over the problems of the day before. Finally, at six o'clock, I got up and went into the living room, where I began writing my opening statement for the press conference that afternoon. In the shattered schedules of the day before, I had not yet had time to focus on that work. I got into the office late and checked on the preparations for the announcement. The staff had done an excellent job in completing the regulations and in writing the lengthy preamble that explained the basis for our decision. The press release was also ready to go. I was told that Sawhill had telephoned, and I returned his call.

John and I first went over his discussion with Russ Train, and discovered that each of us had a slightly different perception of what had been agreed to. John said that he wanted to do some further work with Interior in analyzing the effects of our intended standards in the later years and asked for some information on our numbers. I agreed to get him the data but also made it clear that if he wanted to suggest any changes he would have to discuss it with Train; my intention was to go ahead as planned. We rang off amicably, though at each end of the line there were some unresolved doubts, and I turned back to preparations for the press conference. One of the major lead processors had published a full-page advertisement in the Washington *Post* the day before and in the *New York Times* on Sunday, claiming that removal of lead from gasoline would waste one million barrels of crude oil a day. We considered that claim an outrageous distortion, and I started to gather information so that I could discuss it at the press conference.

Around twelve-thirty I received a telephone call from Jim Tozzi, Sawhill's highly capable staff assistant. Jim explained that, after doing some frenetic work during the morning, Sawhill urgently wanted us to consider a modification to our standards. I could scarcely believe that at this late stage he was proposing a change, but Tozzi read out a series of numbers, which he proposed be substituted for our intended standards. The purpose was to convert the phased program from four years to five years, ending at the fifth year with a standard somewhat more stringent than that originally proposed by EPA. Hurriedly I summoned six or eight of the key staff members from various parts of the agency who had worked on the regulations, and we discussed the proposal. I pointed out that the modified standards would accomplish our basic objectives; not only would they defuse the potentially explosive confrontation with the White House but they would strengthen our defensive position against attacks by the oil industry, and its supporters in Congress, that we were being irresponsible in the face of the sharpening oil crisis. To my surprise, nearly everyone agreed that we should accept the proposal.

Implementing the change required frenzied efforts. The press release had to be retyped and duplicated. The regulations themselves also had to be changed, not only to modify the numbers but to explain why they were changed. Once the paperwork was in progress, I called Russ Train to clear the change with him. This time I caught up with him in Colorado Springs. He had just completed a press conference and was annoyed because he had learned at the press conference that Secretary of the Interior Rogers Morton had just announced initiation of a shale-oil development in Colorado, Wyoming, and Utah, and Russ had not been warned of the announcement. As I had expected, Russ did not object to the modification in our standards and was delighted to learn that with this relatively minor change we had at last emerged from an ugly clash with the White House. I then called Jim Tozzi and a little later also caught John Sawhill and reported to each that we intended to make the changes they had proposed. They too were relieved that we had finally reached a resolution; Sawhill commented, "You wouldn't believe how hard I'm fighting off the wolves with the other hand."

By the time of the press conference at three o'clock I felt as limp as a washcloth. Fortified with several cups of coffee, however, I stepped up before the glaring lights and began to read my opening statement. Vitrually no one in the crowded newsroom realized that making the public announcement and answering reporters' questions were for me an anticlimax after the turmoil I had already been through. The press conference lasted for fifty-five minutes and went quite well; all the technical questions were covered in considerable detail. When I got back upstairs I received another call from Russ Train. By now he was in Denver at our regional office. He had arrived there during the press conference and heard part of it as it was piped in live to an audience there. We both expressed our relief that the regulations were out, and then shifted discussion to a new crisis; there were rumors that the White House planned to send to Congress recommendations proposing a general relaxation in the automobile standards.

A few minutes later I received a phone call from Dick Fairbanks. All friendliness, he apologized for losing his temper. We joked about the press conference and agreed to get together soon for lunch. Though we might bear a few scars, the hatchet was buried quickly. It had to be, and we both knew it. There were too many issues, bubbling up fast, that required our working together to permit any lingering hostility caused by disagreement over a single decision.

It is worth pausing to note several features of the inter-agency review of these lead-in-gas regulations. Although every review is distinctive because the problems are varied, several features of the process we underwent were quite typical. Perhaps the most important is that the final judgment involved a balancing of health risks, costs, and energy penalties, which cannot easily be measured against each other. As usual, basic disagreements existed concerning the severity of the health risks, as well as the fuel penalties that might result from the regulations. It also was entirely typical that the participants in the final round of interagency argument were not experts in these issues. Yet we all argued with vehemence that the questions should be so resolved as to give maximum protection to the concerns within our own spheres of responsibility. Nor was it unusual that as a result of the bargaining process the regulations were modified to provide partial relief for the concerns expressed by the other agencies, though the ultimate effect of the regulations was not substantially changed. This is not always the case. Sometimes the decision swings wholly to one side or the other in the thrashing-out process, but most often there is a bit of give and take.

Perhaps the most important feature of the machinery of government demonstrated by this example is the complexity of the process through which government policy is formulated. This is even more fully appreciated when one recognizes that the final round of argument was only one small episode in the long history of these EPA regulations. The full story began with the initial scientific research into the matter of health hazards caused by lead in the environment. It included the congressional decision in the Clean Air Act of 1970 to authorize EPA to regulate that potential problem. It encompassed several intensive efforts to correlate evidence of brain damage in children with levels of airborne lead in specific localities and to document the precise manner in which lead in gasoline might contribute to health risks. It also covered a vast amount of work to determine the cost and difficulty to the automobile and petroleum industry that would accompany a reduction of lead in gasoline. All of this information was pulled together and balanced out before EPA first proposed its regulations in February 1972 and again when EPA reproposed the regulations in January 1973.

Furthermore, even when the final regulations had been promulgated, the action was by no means concluded. The Ethyl Corporation brought suit to attack the regulations in court, and in December 1974 the Unites States Court of Appeals set them aside. It ruled, over a strong dissent, that EPA had failed to quantify with adequate evidence the adverse impact of lead in gas upon the public health. EPA requested a rehearing, and in April 1976 the court reversed its earlier decision. The regulations finally went into effect.

Conflicts between EPA and the White House have not been limited to disputes over EPA's regulations. They have also cropped up in a broad range of budgetary and legislative issues. Perhaps the sharpest battle broke out in January 1974 over proposed amendments to the Clean Air Act. Amid the pressures brought about by the Arab oil embargo, the beginnings of a recession in the U.S. economy, and the Watergate crisis, a few individuals on the White House staff attempted to force EPA to support sweeping amendments to weaken the requirements of the Clean Air Act. At the peak of the dispute Russ Train declared that he would resign rather than support those amendments. When that word reached higher levels in the White House, the hard line softened and a compromise was worked out. Explosive confrontations like that, however, are rare. Most problems are treated as routine business, and are handled by subordi-

nate staff. The working relationships normally are cooperative, and even friendly. Differences of opinion are common,
but solutions are usually achieved by a mutual recognition
that there has to be some compromise on both sides.

In working out all of these issues with its many critics in
other departments, the White House, and OMB, EPA has
been forced to establish a balance in its decisions. It has had
to be sufficiently sensitive to the economic, social, and other
impacts of the environmental requirements to preserve a
degree of harmony with the rest of the government. This
balance must be maintained. Every government agency is
designed to meet a group of special needs within the country.
This is true of the Departments of Agriculture, Labor,
Commerce, and HEW, and it is true of EPA. Each agency
develops its own constituency, and that constituency exerts
all the political power it can muster to influence the agency
to make decisions that support its special concerns.

These pressures create a set of centrifugal forces within
our government. There has to be a system for keeping the
actions of each part of the government consistent with the
needs of the whole. This is the function that the White House
staff and OMB are designed to serve. Their power, derived
from the President, reflects the fact that the President is the
one person in the entire structure who is elected by the
general public. The system is consistent with the basic
constitutional structure of our democracy which makes government policy responsive to the public will. The task of
maintaining a balance against all the competing special
concerns is essential if the general public interest is to be
protected.

CHAPTER 8

The Water Pollution Bill

AT THE SOUND OF THE BUZZER I walked across to my desk and picked up the telephone. I listened a moment and then repeated aloud my secretary's announcement: "Carl Klein is here and wants to come in to discuss the water pollution amendments." One of the five men sitting at my conference table hopped up and darted into the bathroom, closing the door behind him. "Well," I said, turning back to the telephone, "send him right in." The door opened and in strode the Honorable Carl L. Klein, tall, bald, bulldog-faced, fiftyish, heavy-set; a former mortgage lawyer from the outskirts of Chicago, friend of the late Senator Everett Dirksen, and at that moment, in the month of December 1969, Assistant Secretary of the Interior for Water Quality and Research.

Klein's eyes swept across my office as if he was looking for someone. He gave a perfunctory greeting to the four staff assistants from the Federal Water Pollution Control Administration seated at the table. Then he turned to me, and in a tone half-menacing and half-pleading he asked what we were doing. After hearing my cryptic response and barking out several loosely connected comments, Carl Klein seemed satisfied. He wheeled around abruptly and marched out of my office. The bathroom door then opened and back into the room walked David D. Dominick, short, thirtyish, a Yale graduate, wearing horn-rimmed glasses but smoking a roll-your-own cigarette, former congressional aide, nephew of Colorado Senator Peter Dominick, and at the time Commissioner of the Federal Water Pollution Control Administration.

The game of hide-and-seek played by Dave Dominick and his boss, Carl Klein, reflected the friction in their relationship, which had begun in early 1969, when they had taken over the two top jobs in the federal water pollution control programs. Their personalities clashed right from the start.

I had been asked in the summer of 1969 to join a small group working out of the White House to develop proposals that the President could submit as an Environmental Message to Congress at the start of 1970. My assignment had been to pull together proposals for overhauling the entire framework of the Federal Water Pollution Control Act. Knowing little about the subject, I turned to Dave Dominick, who had responded with a mixture of delight and apprehension. He was pleased that I had asked for his help, but he knew that Klein would discover and resent his involvement in an effort that, for the sake of speed and simplicity, was bypassing the normal chain of command and leaving Carl Klein out of the action. Harboring a few qualms, Dave had assigned four or five of his best assistants to work with me on the project. There then began the process by which the theories of staff within the bureaucracy moved up the line and were forged and hammered into presidential recommendations. The public pressure for environmental reform had been strongly felt in the White House, and almost by reflex action the government turned to the experts within its own ranks to develop the needed response.

The little task force working quietly out of my office on the sixth floor at Interior was only one of many such efforts going on in Washington at the end of 1969. At HEW a similar team was developing proposed amendments to strengthen the air pollution programs, and teams elsewhere were addressing a variety of other environmental needs. On Capitol Hill, legislators were drawing up their own proposals, often taking suggestions from the same sources within the bureaucracy that were sending ideas to the White House. Professional organizations, state agencies, and other outside groups were preparing their own ideas. The winds of change were blowing. New public demands were creating new prospects for legislation, and attention began to focus on the Congress of the United States, which makes the basic decisions on all our government programs.

The water pollution proposals prepared for President Nixon's 1970 Environmental Message were destined to become part of one of the most important legislative struggles of the entire environmental movement. Its climax was the enactment of the Federal Water Pollution Control Act Amendments of 1972, one of the two or three biggest achievements by Congress during the environmental heyday of the early 1970s. The far-reaching impact of that law transformed fundamental features of the national effort to combat water pollution, and the financial cost of the programs it required runs to the tens of billions of dollars.

The President's 1970 Environmental Message was presented to Congress and the country with all the fanfare the White House could command. The message proposed strong measures to control air pollution, water pollution, pesticides, ocean dumping, noise, and many other environmental problems. The usual large White House press conference was supplemented by teams that were sent to brief the reporters and editorial boards in major cities around the country. Briefings were also given to all the principal Congressmen. At one of these briefings, in the small, wood-paneled conference chamber of the Senate Public Works Committee, Dave Dominick carefully enumerated the details of the water pollution proposals to an attentive Edmund Muskie.

Senator Muskie sat a few feet from Dominick around the

corner of the conference table, politely asking questions to be sure he understood all the details. Taking his own notes, he filled page after page of a small committee note pad. Muskie had reason to pay close attention. Not long afterward, he introduced his own bill to revise the water pollution laws and later he would become the chief antagonist of the administration, taking issue with its provisions in the amendments. In February 1970, however, that struggle still lay far ahead, farther, in fact, than any of us then would have imagined.

Despite the emphasis given the water pollution proposals by the President's Environmental Message, despite the widespread congressional recognition of the need for these changes, and despite strong public pressure for across-the-board environmental reform, the proposals were destined to sit on the sidelines for an entire year before receiving any serious legislative attention. This had nothing to do with their merits. The House Public Works Committee, which had a crowded schedule, decided not to take up the bills until the Senate Public Works Committee was also prepared to address them. The Senate committee held fourteen days of public hearings on the eighteen water pollution bills before it but decided to tackle air pollution first. This, it turned out, consumed the whole of 1970, and the Ninety-first Congress adjourned in December with the water pollution bills still waiting in line.

When the new Congress convened at the start of 1971, it turned its attention immediately to the revisions proposed for the Federal Water Pollution Control Act. The President again submitted proposals similar to those sent up a year before. Individual Senators and Congressmen filed a stream of other proposals. EPA had just been formed and environmental concern was still rising throughout the country, assuring the momentum of public support for strong legislation. People wanted no more of fishkills, contaminated water, and stench-filled river valleys. Having enacted the Clean Air Act of 1970, the Senate Public Works Committee and its Subcommittee on Air and Water Pollution stood ready to tackle the water bill as a first order of business. Leon Billings, Senator Muskie's aide, grandly predicted the completion of Senate action by the end of March.

The subcommittee held preliminary hearings in early February to review the existing programs. In mid-March it began hearings on the proposed new legislation. These hearings gave notice to the world that the subcommittee was going to work on the water pollution bills. Letters, telephone calls, and requests for meetings and visits poured in from all groups concerned with the bills. It was a critical period, one in which the basic themes of the new legislation were to be given shape. Each member of the subcommittee and its staff was exposed to comment from every quarter, and their composite impressions would dictate their basic approach to the pending legislation.

Reviewing all these comments consumed several months. Then came a second phase in the legislative process. On June 4 the subcommittee met for its first executive session to begin that process of debates, drafting, argument, and counterproposal through which the detailed provisions of a major bill are put together. Withdrawing unto itself, the subcommittee spent the next two months in intensive work, developing a new draft bill comprehensively amending the water pollution act.

Back at EPA, I had little knowledge of what course the subcommittee was following. Occasionally a few clues would slip out, but nothing clear or conclusive. We knew only that the subcommittee was engaged in a process by which the conflicting personal opinions of its members had to be incorporated into a single bill that all members could support. Senator Muskie, of course, had a dominant voice. His role as sponsor of the Clean Air Act and his emerging strength as a contender for the presidency in 1972 added to the stature he automatically possessed as chairman of the subcommittee. For several years Muskie had been the most outspoken advocate in the Congress for stronger pollution control requirements. A balancing force was Jennings Randolph, chairman of the full Public Works Committee and one of the Senate's senior members. Randolph was from West Virginia, where the need for attracting industry and building employment had been considered more urgent than protection of environmental quality, and his chief efforts within the committee had been directed toward pushing for highway construction and other public works, which provided jobs and signified progress. He was more conservative in his outlook than Senator Muskie, but the two of them had always seemed to find a common ground. The ranking Republican was Howard Baker of Tennessee, the fast-rising son-in-law of the late Senator Dirksen. Baker had the smiling-but-earnest manner of a well-polished country boy. He also had a quick understanding of environmental issues and a good grasp of legislative detail. Two newcomers to the committee who were to play significant roles were Senators John Tunney and James Buckley. Tunney, son of the boxing champion Gene Tunney, was a youthful Californian with liberal Democratic views who had won election with a campaign based on the Kennedy style of glamour politics. Buckley, by contrast, precise and intellectual, had won in a three-way election in New York, running on the Conservative Party ticket. Despite the differences in personality and political outlook of its members, the Public Works Committee had a record of working together smoothly. Its approach, of necessity, had to include compromise. This meant that any bill developed by the committee would reflect a conciliation of all the conflicting points of view.

In early August the subcommittee issued its proposed new bill and sent it to the full committee. It was immediately clear that the bill was adapted to the changing public attitudes; it would tremendously strengthen the pollution control programs. One of its most striking provisions required that all waters everywhere be cleaned of pollution by 1980 to permit swimming and to protect fish and shellfish. As soon as this draft was circulated, the battle heated up. Environmentalists generally were delighted, but industry attacked the "swimmable waters" standard as unrealistic. The deluge of comments and criticism sent the Senate working group back into closed sessions. Once again I wondered what decisions the committee was making.

It was not until early October that the committee neared completion of its work. Final drafts of the bill were circulated among the Senators and their staffs, although disputes remained over a very few issues. When members of our staff succeeded in obtaining copies of the bill and brought them back to EPA, we had our first chance to find out what was happening. We read the bill eagerly — and we were amazed. The Senate committee had gone even further than it had in the August draft toward tightening radically the water pollution statutes.

On October 19 the committee voted unanimously to report out the bill and send it to the floor of the Senate for approval. The action was announced with a burst of publicity, including grandiloquent statements that the bill would assure the achievement of clean water throughout the United States. Environmentalists hailed it enthusiastically. Editorials roared their endorsements. Almost immediately, there was a national drive to urge rapid passage of the bill.

The committee's report issued a call for revolutionary change. It concluded that "the national effort to abate and control water pollution has been inadequate in every vital aspect," the task of setting water quality standards was "lagging," the lack of adequate funding to construct sewage treatment plants was "causing critical problems," and there had been "an almost total lack of enforcement." The committee also found that many of the nation's navigable waters were severely polluted and that major waterways near industrial and urban areas were "unfit for most purposes." On the basis of these determinations, the committee evidently had decided to make a sharp break with the past. It had rewritten the law of water pollution control to a degree far exceeding anyone's expectation.

In response to criticism of the "swimmable waters" standard, the committee had reduced and qualified its role, but as a replacement the committee had inserted a whole new set of pollution control requirements. These required every industrial plant to install the best equipment technology could devise to control its pollution. (This was known as "the best practicable control technology" standard.) The dramatic innovation was that these requirements were imposed absolutely; unlike all prior standards, there was no requirement for evidence that such control was needed to protect water quality in the receiving waters. The committee evidently felt that those requirements had provided too many opportunities for polluters to dodge and delay. The new standards also reflected the growing belief that even in the absence of proven harm there should be no right to pollute the public waterways. In fact, the bill proceeded to an even stronger requirement, pushing all industries to eliminate their discharges entirely (or to achieve "zero discharge") in a second stage of control, to be achieved where possible by 1981. It nailed that down by declaring it national policy to eliminate the discharge of pollutants by 1985.

Though copies of the bill were difficult to obtain and the committee's report on the bill was not to be printed until October 28, popular support was overwhelming. The bill was pushed ahead through the procedural formalities and came up for a vote on November 2. There was little time for discussion. During the floor debate no challenge was made to any of the pollution control standards or other major features of the bill. In the fall of 1971, no one was about to speak out against clean water. When the final vote came after only brief consideration, the Senate passed the bill by a thumping, unanimous vote of 86 to 0.

Then the counterattack began. The publicity given to the stringent requirements of the Senate bill, especially the provisions to achieve zero discharge, triggered a powerful reaction from several large groups. The intensity of that reaction was heightened by the swift and unanimous passage of the bill by the full Senate and by predictions that the bill might be approved by the House in short order. As the provisions of the Senate bill became better understood, anxieties increased to an almost near-panic level. Nearly every industry dumping its waste into rivers and lakes suddenly feared it would be put out of business, or at least forced to spend astronomical sums. During the long months the committee had been working on the bill, few outsiders knew what was being drafted. Now here was a massive document of intricate detail — when published in a double-spaced printed format, it stretched out for a benumbing 188 pages — and to many, its provisions brought shock and dismay.

Three interests among all others were most severely affected. They were industry, the federal budget, and the state pollution control programs. The possible danger to industry was obvious in the multitude of strict new standards exemplified by the zero-discharge goal. The damage threatened to the federal budget lay in the huge increases in spending contained in the bill. Whereas the President's bill at the start of the year had proposed a three-year program of construction grants totaling $6 billion to build sewage treatment plants, the Senate bill jacked that up to a four-year program costing $14 billion, and the bill locked in that spending by special provisions to prevent the funds from being reduced in the annual appropriations. The bill also contained a number of other spending increases that exceeded the administration's proposals. The challenge to state agencies arose both from the new standards and from the provisions establishing a national permit program. By switching over to "best practicable control" everywhere and pushing toward zero discharge, the bill jettisoned the entire existing structure of state water quality standards. In addition, the bill gave EPA power to control the permit program through which the new standards would be applied. Through the extension of federal jurisdiction to all waterways and a number of other provisions, the bill further expanded the federal role in pollution control, and state officials didn't like it.

The White House reacted to the Senate bill with an all-bells alarm. The Nixon Administration's concern for the welfare of American industry, its commitment to strengthening state government, and its apprehension over growth in the federal budget were all menaced by the three basic areas in which the most sweeping changes were proposed by the Senate bill.

Two days after the Senate vote, White House officials met with representatives of seven trade associations to plan the strategy for a counterattack. The next day about thirty executives from major industries were called together by Secretary of Commerce Maurice Stans to be briefed on the provisions of the bill. With similar speed state officials also answered the call to arms. A national conference of these officials was being held in Boston the day after the Senate vote; following heated discussion they passed a resolution condemning the bill and agreed to seek help from their governors.

The first tactic decided upon by opponents of the Senate bill was to try to make the House Public Works Committee reopen hearings on the legislation it had held earlier in the year. Unless there were new hearings to provide a forum for criticism, it would be difficult for the critics to prevent swift acceptance of the Senate bill. The White House, therefore, decided to go public with an all-out, frontal assault. On November 9, Ronald Ziegler, presidential press secretary, announced that the White House strongly opposed many provisions of the Senate bill and would seek to have the House Public Works Committee reopen its hearings and fully reconsider the legislation. The days that followed witnessed that type of frenetic activity on Capitol Hill that accompanies important legislative decisions. Lobbyists from many quarters tried to persuade the House committee not to swallow the Senate bill. Countless meetings, telephone calls, letters, resolutions, and press releases were part of the massive effort.

The House Public Works Committee was a very different body from its Senate counterpart. Reflecting the general differences between the two bodies as entities, the House committee members were less swayed by swings of opinion in the media and the press. They tended to be somewhat more sympathetic to the concerns of industry, more committed to the roles of state government, and generally more conservative in their personal political beliefs. Our contacts quickly revealed that most members of the House committee felt the Senate bill had gone overboard on many points.

Despite their personal opinions, many members of the House committee were hesitant about making major changes in the legislation. They knew that if the House committee weakened the pollution control requirements, they would be portrayed as selling out to special interests. Many members already felt resentful that on past occasions the Senate committee had assumed the hero's role in public by adopting excessively tough pollution control requirements, forcing the House committee to take the heat for modifying its proposals. Certainly John Blatnik, the House committee chairman, felt this resentment. He had championed stronger water pollution programs as far back as the 1956 act, but in recent years had been overshadowed by Senator Muskie. Sensitive over his position, Blatnik opposed reopening the hearings. Normally Blatnik's attitude might have been the one that prevailed, but a fateful event intervened. Just as the issue was coming to a head John Blatnik suffered a heart attack, which removed him from the battle. A few days later the committee scheduled four days of hearings to be held from December 7 to 10.

As opponents of the Senate bill sharpened their knives, the most telling criticisms focused on the cost of achieving the proposed standards. Roberta Hornig of the Washington *Star* told me that she had talked to several Democratic, liberal economists, and even they felt that forcing everyone to achieve zero discharge would waste billions of dollars with no discernible environmental benefit. In addition, since some of the materials now dumped in the waterways would have to go somewhere, there would be great burdens on land, air, and energy consumption. On the first day of hearings, Bill Ruckelshaus emphasized that setting unrealistic statutory standards would undermine respect for the government. Witness after witness attacked the cost of the standards. State officials criticized the disruption of their programs and the federal takeover of control. The most forceful witness was Nelson Rockefeller, Governor of New York; he said that his experts estimated that the cost of achieving the 1985 no-discharge standard would hit the figure of $230 billion in New York alone, and by extrapolation he suggested that the national total would be in the range of $2 or $3 trillion.

All this testimony slowed the momentum of the Senate bill. When the hearings ended there was little doubt that the House committee would make substantial changes. What did come as a surprise was the speed with which the committee acted. It went into "mark-up" promptly on December 14, made its decisions on central issues the following night, and held a press conference on December 17. The committee members announced a long list of changes they would make in the Senate bill, leaving to staff the task of working out suitable language.

The House committee accepted the basic format of the Senate bill, but tinkered with many of the details with an effect reminiscent of the Gilbert and Sullivan suggestion that a great deal can be changed by simply inserting the word *not*. It retained the 1976 best practicable control technology standard but allowed EPA to grant two-year extensions where needed. It also kept the more stringent 1981 standards and, in a slightly diluted form, the 1985 no-discharge goal, but it added a vital condition. It required that the National Academy of Sciences undertake a study as to their cost and desirability, and — this was the hitch — it specified that neither the 1981 standards nor the 1985 goal should be implemented until Congress had received the study and once again enacted legislation reaffirming the 1981 and 1985 requirements.

The House committee established a special permit program to be operated by the Corps of Engineers, more friendly than EPA, for disposal of dredged spoil. It provided a special mechanism through which power plants and other plants producing thermal discharges could be relieved from compliance with the full requirements of the act. In response to the complaints of state officials, the committee greatly restricted the role of EPA in administering the permit program.

The only issue on which the White House lost ground was the one on which it had stood alone — the federal budget. Balancing its many other changes, all of which weakened the bill, the House committee substantially increased the federal funding. It jumped the construction grants program from $14 billion all the way up to $20 billion, increasing the federal share to 75 percent of project costs, and also adopted a number of other provisions for increasing federal spending.

After the December 17 press conference, Congress went home for Christmas and the water pollution bill went into hibernation for nearly three additional months while the House Public Works Committee staff developed language for its bill and its report explaining the changes. These did not come out until March 11, but in the meantime environmentalists had been hard at work. At a March 6 press conference, a coalition of twenty-five groups, including the League of Women Voters, Common Cause, several major labor unions, and nearly all of the large environmental organizations, announced that it would push for amendments to reinstate the Senate provisions when the water bill came up for action on the House floor. It was a tactic some of the older environmental leaders felt was doomed to failure, with a likely result of polarizing and antagonizing the House Committee leadership. But the attempt was undertaken with full publicity and intensive lobbying efforts. John Dingell and Henry Reuss, two of the staunchest environmentalists in the House, sponsored the amendments, and a sizable number of Congressmen promised their support. When the bill reached the floor at the end of March, however, the proposals of the environmentalists were defeated by solid majorities voting to support the decisions of the House committee.

The reaction of environmentalists to the extensive changes made by the House Public Works Committee and to the decisive defeat of their amendments on the House floor was dejection and hostility. The popular expectations of a strong water pollution bill had turned sour, and many of the youthful leaders whom I talked with began to propose waiting until the next session of Congress for a more favorable attitude to their problem. "Better no bill than the House bill," they commented derisively. For a moment the prospects teetered indecisively. Environmentalists were disillusioned by the actions taken in the House; industry and state officials were dissatisfied even by those revisions; and the White House was boiling over the increases in federal spending. We in EPA were suddenly faced with the possibility that the whole act might be rejected.

We had reason to be anxious. The problems of running existing water pollution programs had mounted because of the long delays and the uncertainty over what the new legislation would be. We felt an urgent need for the improvements provided by the new bill, many of which were not at all controversial. Now it appeared that, because of disputes over a few major issues, the whole set of needed amendments might be delayed another year or two. To me that prospect was frightening; the permit program begun under the Refuse Act was entirely stalled, awaiting the new law.

Throughout the country industrial plants were pouring pollutants into rivers and lakes. The condition of the water was deplorable, and getting worse. In many industrial areas the very names of local rivers had become synonymous with open sewers. The heavy volumes of wastes, as they decomposed in the water, depleted the oxygen needed to sustain aquatic life. Chemical compounds and other toxic substances had lethal effects on fish and shellfish. Thick beds of sludge had formed on many lake bottoms, and on occasion particles would bubble to the surface, emitting horrible odors. Despite the public outcry against such offensive conditions, many companies refused to undertake cleanup programs until the federal law was enacted. It was not fair, they claimed with some justice, for them to make major investments to reduce their pollution before they knew what the legal requirements were going to be. Similar factors were delaying construction of municipal sewage treatment plants. Since the pending legislation promised higher federal grants, local governments were waiting for the new law before going ahead with their projects. The uncertainty in Congress, therefore, was holding back needed efforts everywhere to clean up nasty water pollution problems.

One of the deepest frustrations was that there was so little we could do to influence the outcome in Congress. We knew that White House attitudes ranged from mixed to hostile, and we agreed with a number of the objections to the Senate bill, but we desperately needed a new bill. In late May I was to give a speech in Washington. I was caught between loyalty owed to the President who had appointed me and loyalty owed to the program I was working for, but I knew that my ultimate loyalty was owed to the public and that the right course was simply to address the issues as I saw them. I argued as strongly as I could that the similarities between the Senate and House bills far overshadowed their differences; and I urged that all groups should work to find a compromise, pointing out that we were facing a calamity unless new legislation was enacted during that session of Congress. That speech attracted only scant attention, but fortunately the argument began to gain a growing acceptance. Once again there was public pressure to push ahead with the water pollution legislation.

In mid-May a conference committee of representatives from the Senate and House Public Works Committees began the tedious task of resolving differences between the two bills. At this point the legislators again went behind closed doors, and month after month went by as they continued their deliberations. Since 1972 was a presidential election year, the summer was interrupted by recesses for the Democratic and Republican National Conventions. Moving by fits and starts, the conference committee slowly worked through one large section of the bill after another. Periodically some hint about its approach on certain issues would seep out of the committee, but it was not enough for us to form a reasonable idea of the shape of the bill.

When the first of September brought reports that a

number of issues were still unresolved, we became seriously alarmed that the legislation might not be enacted, especially as it was now rumored that President Nixon might veto the bill. Finally, in the last week of September, the conference committee completed the last of its thirty-nine executive sessions and unanimously approved a bill to be resubmitted to the House and Senate for final approval.

The conference committee bill contained compromises on nearly all of the major differences. On the heated issue of standards, it re-established the two-phased structure proposed by the Senate, but with several modifications. The bill retained the existing state water quality standards and combined them with the technology standards in a manner established by the House bill. On several issues, including provisions for the permit program and the disposal of dredged material, the conference committee devised a complex arrangement striking a balance between the Senate and House versions. On the critical issue of funding the construction grants program, however, the conference committee in effect adopted the higher figures of the House and established a three-year program costing $18 billion (Congress having already voted $2 billion for the current year in the interim). Other spending programs authorized by the bill brought its price tag to the staggering total of $24.6 billion.

The funding provisions sparked the only major lobbying effort after the conference committee bill was reported. The White House accepted all provisions but the mandatory commitment of $18 billion for construction grants; it made a desperate, last-minute effort to obtain relief from this program. The mixed record of the legislative history of the grants gave rise to a bitter controversy when, a few months later, there was a presidential impoundment of these funds.

With congressional adjournment expected weekly in anticipation of the national election, then less than two months away, completion of the water pollution bill became a down-to-the-wire race. The conference committee bill was over-whelmingly approved by both houses of Congress on October 4 and sent to the President. Most outsiders assumed that President Nixon would not veto a bill with such immense political appeal so soon before Election Day, but inside the administration the merits of a veto were being debated in earnest. Bill Ruckelshaus sent the President a confidential letter strongly urging that the bill be signed and contending that the objections on funding were overstated by the bill's opponents. A week later, I was with Ruckelshaus in California in the Sacramento Airport when his name was called out on the public address system. As I watched him through the glass door of a telephone booth, I could see his face reflect agitation and dismay: his letter to the President had leaked to the press, causing an immediate sensation. The letter aligned Ruckelshaus with the President's opponents in bringing public pressure against the President to sign the bill.

Back in Washington the tensions surrounding the climax were rising. Congress was on the eve of adjournment. Racing against the clock, with the national elections now only three weeks off, both the Senate and the House were pushing through a crush of major legislation. The President had not yet acted on the water pollution bill, but it was his tenth day and the bill would become law unless he vetoed it.

At this last moment the water pollution bill was caught up in an even bigger storm. One of the other important bills being considered by Congress was a proposal to give the President authority to impose tight controls on total federal spending. When the Senate rejected that proposal in a late evening vote, the President responded by vetoing the water pollution bill. In a public statement issued just before midnight, he declared, "Even if the Congress defaults its obligations to the taxpayers — I shall not default mine."

The President's action was challenged by the Senate the very next morning with an immediate move to override the veto. It carried easily by a vote of 52 to 12. The question now was whether the bill would be voted on by the House in the closing hours before it adjourned. That same afternoon the House took up the measure and it too overrode the veto. The 1972 water pollution bill was no longer a bill — it was a law!

The close timing of the water pollution bill became dramatically clear a few hours later. On the next major issue raised for action, an important transportation bill, the House could not obtain a quorum, and it adjourned for the year, leaving the transportation measure and many other important bills unfinished. After three years of gestation, including twenty months of active congressional deliberation, the Federal Water Pollution Control Act Amendments of 1972 were finally enacted into law on October 18, 1972. One day later, and it would have been too late!

Every bill that runs the gamut of procedural steps necessary for enactment by Congress has its unique legislative history. The vicissitudes of a single bill can never reflect the range of actions that occur daily in the congressional process. Still, the history of the water pollution bill reveals several features of our legislative process.

One extremely interesting point to note is that throughout the lengthy three-year process several important provisions of the bill were never significantly changed. General agreement existed from the outset that the federal enforcement procedures needed to be streamlined and strengthened. Proposals to authorize EPA to bring prompt actions against violators, to seek court orders, and to impose fines were hardly changed and only little debated from their initiation by the administration through their adoption by the Senate, the House, the conference committee, and Congress acting as a whole. Similarly, the important new provisions to authorize citizen suits to enforce provisions of the law were generally agreed to throughout the process and finally enacted with essentially the same terms as had been initially proposed. Many other provisions fell in this category. These provisions all had major importance to the program and overwhelming support, but they became captive to the rest of the water pollution bill; their implementation was delayed for a year and a half while other provisions were debated, and they would have been delayed indefinitely if for any reason the bill had not been enacted.

There was another category of provisions, which swelled as the bill moved step by step through the legislative process. This was most evident in the spending features, particularly the sewage treatment plant construction grants program. The administration proposed that it be increased to $6 billion; the Senate jumped that to $14 billion; and the House raised it up to $20 billion. This tendency to raise the stakes appeared in the provisions for federal grants to support state agency programs. The original administration bill proposed funding these grants at $15 million initially, increasing the sum to $30 million three years later. The Senate bill authorized $30 million at the start, to rise to $40 million in subsequent years. The House bill set the figure at $60 million, to rise to $75 million. It came as no surprise that the conference committee, in its generosity, adopted the provisions of the House bill. In the dynamics of legislation the proponents of a bill often seem to stumble over each other in dishing out federal money.

A similar feature is the way that bills grow more complicated as they move through the congressional process, picking up new provisions at each point along the way. Part of this snowballing effect arises from the scrambling of narrow interest groups. Both the dredging industry and the electric power industry, for example, succeeded in obtaining special provisions in the House committee, modifying the impact of the law on their interests.

Through the cumbersome process of Senate committee–House committee–conference committee, the need to reach a consensus on the entire bill tortures many provisions into complication. Issues are often settled by the legislators (or their aides) using language that both sides can accept though each may have different ideas as to what it means — a procedure that may sacrifice the coherence of the bill. The Senate bill, for example, set forth a logical approach, placing dominant authority over the new national permit program in the federal EPA. The House bill set forth a different but equally logical approach, transferring chief responsibility to the state agencies. The compromise reached by the conference committee was a jumble of both, providing for the program to be transferred to state agencies within roughly five months but subject to a long list of statutory prerequisites that most states were unable to satisfy for years.

Another striking feature in the development of the water pollution bill was the unanimous approval by the United States Senate of the zero-discharge provisions in the Senate bill. The potentially astronomical costs of meeting these standards were, of course, loudly denounced by the critics. Their cost figures were attacked by the bill's proponents as speculative and highly suspect, but the most striking revelation of all was that those who originated the standards and those who approved them had no estimates at all of what the costs might be.

What the zero-discharge standards really indicated was a new attitude toward our natural waterways, namely, that their use as a receptacle for manmade wastes is intolerable and that, in short, no one has the right to pollute. The Senate committee accepted this attitude as a policy judgment, and wrote it into the bill with little evaluation of the practical consequences. In retrospect, the zero-discharge requirements of the original Senate bill now appear hopelessly unrealistic. They illustrate the tendency of the pendulum of public opinion to swing to extremes and the danger that excessive measures may be adopted under the pressure of protest movements. The major changes made by the House committee to soften those requirements made them more realistic and illustrated the advantage of having two houses in the Congress to assure more careful review before requirements are enacted into law.

Any review of the workings of Congress would have to recognize the peculiarities of its intricate process. Oddities and weaknesses in the laws enacted can easily be found. Yet from a broader perspective the history of the Federal Water Pollution Control Act Amendments of 1972 reveals that Congress did act effectively to set new directions in national policy that were responsive to the needs felt throughout the country. The provisions to establish more stringent abatement standards, to increase federal funds, to impose tight deadlines, to establish a national permit program, and to strengthen federal enforcement all represented a broad consensus that crystallized during the lengthy congressional process. Through all the checks and balances, the system functioned effectively to translate public opinion into national public policy.

That system of checks and balances, however, severely restricts the freedom of Congress to act. Throughout the system, it is much easier to block a bill than to advance one. This forces all action into a consensus mode, in which dozens of individuals become critical to enactment and hundreds or even thousands may influence the bill's terms. The process is not suited to swift or decisive action. It requires the momentum of powerful support to push a bill all the way through to passage, overcoming inertia and all varieties of large or petty opposition. Not only must there be agreement that there is a need for congressional action to deal with a serious problem, there must be agreement on just what the action should be. And this can delay enactment by Congress until long after the need is obvious.

The long history of the water pollution bill is only one

example of the time it takes for Congress to act. Countless others would serve as well. One example is the toxic substances bill. Proposed by the administration in February of 1971 to provide authority for EPA to require testing of chemicals before they are introduced in the marketplace, this legislation was passed by both the Senate and the House during 1973, and the bills went to a conference committee to resolve differences. Unable to agree on compromises, the conference committee adjourned in December 1973 and did not meet until well past the middle of 1974. The Ninety-second Congress adjourned at the end of 1974 without passing the bill. Although the need for legislation to deal with dangers from toxic substances has been formally recognized by both the House and the Senate as well as the administration, disagreement over what provisions the law should contain have prevented its enactment. For five long years the need has remained unattended.

The responsiveness of the legislative process to strong swings in public opinion was reflected by the Senate water pollution bill, though in the time required for enactment temporary swings of public opinion are likely to be evened out. The need for a sustained push to achieve legislation thus provides a benefit in partially isolating the enactment process from fluctuations in public opinion. It permits a slower and more stable evolution of national policy. It permits weaknesses to be revealed as proposals are fully debated. The wheels of God grind slowly, and so do those of Congress.

CHAPTER 9

The Brokerage of Policy

THE LAST THREE CHAPTERS described individual episodes in the federal government's response to the environmental crisis. One was the development of a program (the permit program) within a federal agency; another the thrashing out of a decision (the lead-in-gas regulations) between the agency and the White House; and the third the enactment of a law (the water pollution act) by the Congress. Each reveals the complexity of government action, and the hidden sets of checks and balances that restrain its action. Before proceeding with the story of the environmental movement and EPA, it may be appropriate for me to pause briefly to relate these descriptions of how things happen in the government to the underlying questions of *why* they happen.

The formation of government policy is not an event but a process. It takes place over a period of time and involves legions of participants, who may never see or know each other. From a distance, governmental action may appear to be the work of a handful of influential members of Congress or perhaps the head of a federal agency. On closer look that image fractures into a thousand pieces.

The real policy of the government must be tested by what is done, not what is said. The policy on controlling pollution from steel mills, for instance, must be found in what degree of control individual mills are actually required to achieve. Those requirements are the end product of a long process of policy formation. It includes the passage of laws by Congress, the issuance of regulations by an agency head, the determination of specific requirements by on-the-scene officials, and the approach taken toward enforcement. No one person controls the total policy. No single decision can be more than a small ingredient in the total approach.

Even when one looks only at the big policy decisions made by the EPA Administrator, close inspection reveals that that man does not have nearly as much real power as he appears to have under the laws and in the press clippings. The most powerful officials are subject to many constraints that limit their actual ability to control the policies they announce or approve. The most immediate constraint is the limits of time, and these limits necessitate a great amount of delegation. Thus grows the role of staff and subordinates.

A more profound limitation on the exercise of power by chief officials is the fact that each decision is only one piece of a much bigger puzzle. It must fit in with the other pieces. Any decision by the EPA Administrator must conform to the statutory requirements imposed by Congress, as well as to the policy dictates of the White House. The Administrator's discretion is also curbed by practical considerations — factors of cost, technical determinations, or the limits of EPA's budget or manpower. Hemmed in by all sorts of factors beyond his control as he faces one problem after another, the high government official becomes harried. He struggles to find solutions that will accommodate all the conflicting factors, and he spends endless time and energy trying to persuade others to support his solutions.

Pushing hard against every official as he grapples with these problems are all the forces of political pressure. The various pressures reflect the demands of the general public and of all the special interest groups. On basic issues of national policy these political pressures exert force directly on the top officials; they achieve an even greater impact by the way they intrude into all the checks and balances affecting subordinate officials throughout the total government structure.

Looking down over the New York Stock Exchange, one sees a swirling mob of people rushing through the motions of their work. The transactions they carry out represent the lifeblood of the nation's economy. They may affect what types of jobs will be provided, what products made, what cities grow, and what industries flourish. It would be easy to suppose that the men on the floor hold enormous power over the development of the economy, and it is true that their decisions can have profound importance. Yet it would be a mistake to conclude that these few people hold the real power over what happens in our economy. For the most part they are only brokers. They act as representatives of others who are out of sight, and the transactions they carry out simply manifest the judgments of those who do have power.

The analogy of the stock market is worth keeping in mind when one evaluates the role of the "decision makers" in the nation's capital. To be sure, the scene in Washington has all the exciting bustle. It is where the principal actions in the formation of public policy take place. One can easily be deceived by this appearance of power into believing that vast authority is exercised by the persons holding high government positions. No doubt it is true that their decisions can control the outcome of individual cases, and that their opinions can influence basic policy, especially in the short run. Moving just beneath the surface, however, are currents of political force that mold that basic policy in ways these individuals have no power to resist.

As issues are debated by advocates of opposing positions, the answers that emerge reflect the balance of political strength among different groups within the society. The real power is diffused down and out through the total political system. It does not lie, except in the representative sense, with the top officials, who may hold the legal authority. Their role is important but limited: it is to negotiate the resolution of issues, to carry out a brokerage of policy formation.

Once we recognize that the dominant political power in our government does not rest with the officials who appear to exercise it, we are led to ask where it does lie. There is no single answer. The real power lies in the total grouping of all the different people and forces able to exert pressure through all the different mechanisms of our political system.

To analyze how these forces played on the environmental movement it may be best to begin with the record of results. There can be no question that during the period from 1969 through 1972 our national policy shifted emphatically toward greater efforts to control pollution. This shift was evident in every part of the federal government — in actions by Congress, by the White House, and throughout the executive branch, and even in decisions by the courts. This shift did not occur because a few high officials suddenly decided that environmental problems needed more attention. As we have seen, national policy changed direction because there was a powerful new force of political pressure abroad in the land, and all the brokers of policy responded to its commands.

Government policy is supposed to speak for the public interest. The question is: Does it do so? The environmental movement offers a test example. Many of the sharpest battles in the politics of the environment have pitted environmentalists against American industry. Before looking at the strengths of the environmental movement, we must note the obvious advantages industry has had — obvious at first glance, that is — in this competition. The economic strength of the dominant industrial groups makes it easy for them to finance bold efforts to tell their side of the story. This advantage shows up in many ways.

Lobbying is perhaps the clearest example of industry's

financial leverage. Environmental groups have been able to maintain only a handful of full-time active lobbyists in Washington. Their efforts are curtailed by a restriction in the tax law that prohibits lobbying by organizations that receive tax-deductible, charitable gifts. Industry, by contrast, is represented in Washington by a vast aggregation of trade associations, corporate lawyers, and other agents, whose salaries are deductible from corporate income as ordinary business expenses and therefore are not subject to taxation.

Public advertising is another field where corporate money talks. Skillful advertising can go a long way to mold public opinion. Both environmentalists and industry have relied on advertising to push their cause, but the opportunities are far from equal. In 1974, for instance, the American Electric Power Company went public in a campaign to challenge EPA's policy of requiring the use of scrubbers to control sulfur pollutants and also to challenge federal coal-leasing policies. It published a series of over thirty full-page ads, most of which ran in the *New York Times,* the *Wall Street Journal,* the Washington *Post, Time, Newsweek, U.S. News & World Report, Business Week,* and in almost all local daily and weekly newspapers throughout large portions of the Midwest. The cost for this one campaign was over $3 million.

Another advantage of industry seldom noticed by the public is its ability to present technical information to support its arguments before Congress or EPA. Many decisions rest on disputes over cost, technology, or scientific evidence. Industry usually has ready access to this information and can hire the best experts in the country. Environmentalists generally must rely on limited or volunteer help and often have little ability even to question the data submitted by industry.

A fourth area of advantage to industry is litigation. Questions of national policy are frequently determined by court orders. Industry almost always can afford litigation if it thinks a suit may be helpful, and it can hire the best and most expensive lawyers to argue its case. Environmental organizations are usually strapped for funds. They have won a large number of striking court victories, but they have overcome tremendous odds in doing so.

It might appear that industrial groups have all the advantages and environmentalists have none, which makes one wonder how it ever happened that tough regulatory requirements have been imposed on industry to force it to undertake expensive efforts for pollution control. The answer lies chiefly in the force of public opinion.

The actual public need for pollution control was only marginally more serious in the early 1970s than it had been in the preceding decades. Yet public policy underwent a vast change. What happened? For long years groups concerned with environmental abuse had been gathering strength to assault the prevailing public policy. Conservation organizations were growing in membership. Small government programs were developing. Information was being collected. Members of the press were learning about the problems. Meanwhile, the problems were steadily growing worse. Then awareness of the abuse burst upon the national consciousness, generating irresistible demands for change. The "environmental crisis" was a happening in the arena of public opinion, and the achievements of environmental reform stand as testimony to the political power of public opinion once its fury is unleashed.

A vital factor in the emergence of these strong forces of public opinion has been the growth of organizations committed to achieving environmental reform. At the grassroots level, thousands of different organizations began to work for environmental objectives. Private citizens, often with no experience in government or politics, became forceful, effective leaders, working long hours without pay to mobilize their friends and neighbors to press for environmental protection. These groups quickly became sophisticated in the lobbying techniques of mass meetings, visits to legislators, and letter-writing campaigns, and they rallied citizens to action. Their persuasive influence on political leaders has been heightened by the fact that they worked as volunteers.

Several aggressive new organizations have also emerged at the national level. They have included shoestring lobbying groups like the Environmental Policy Center and Friends of the Earth, and public interest law groups like the Sierra Club Legal Defense Fund, the Natural Resources Defense Council, and the Environmental Defense Fund. These groups not only worked in the campaigns to achieve new legislation but have followed up with dogged dedication to watch over the administration of environmental laws after they were enacted. They have largely been staffed by idealistic young people in their twenties or early thirties, receiving limited salaries and working out of modest and cluttered offices. These new organizations have augmented the efforts of the large membership organizations, such as the National Wildlife Federation, the National Audubon Society, the Wilderness Society, the Izaak Walton League, and the Sierra Club.

Overcoming industry's advantages in staff and financial support, a small number of individuals in these various public interest groups have exerted a profound influence on the enactment and also on the implementation of environmental laws. Through detailed analyses of proposed regulations and administrative decisions, together with a full readiness to contest aggressively everything they disagree with, these groups have functioned with remarkable effectiveness as a counterbalance to the representatives of industry.

As public interest in environmental issues grew, its impact on government policy was strengthened by newspaper and television coverage. Active scrutiny by the press has a subtle but strong effect on government action. Reporters not only report the news, but — just by their presence — they influence what the news will be. Top government officials invariably consider how their actions will be regarded by those who are watching. Awareness of the watchful eye of press adds another dimension to every problem. The more intensively the press covers an issue, the more that issue is brought to the attention of the general public, and the more the general public is likely to assert its interest in it. In response, government policy automatically shifts toward what the general public wants as political leaders compete to obtain "good press" by embracing popular positions.

The spontaneous force of grassroots public opinion, the aggressive leadership by environmental organizations, the constant attention by the press — each of these factors was critical to the driving power of the environmental movement, but what was most important was the way these different forces interacted with each other to produce a cumulative effect. Public opinion was stirred up by press reports to demand environmental reform, but the intensifying press coverage occurred only in response to a quickened public interest.

It is only in the context of intense public interest that the extraordinary effectiveness of the small, often amateurish, national environmental organizations can be understood. By acquiring a detailed knowledge of environmental problems, their young leaders were able to make impressive statements, which were widely reported in the press. The reason they received broad press coverage was that there was strong public concern, and the environmental leaders buttressed that concern by their assertions. Their access to the press gave them clout in all their dealings with government officials, who often also fed them information because of their shared objectives. What really created the political power of the young environmental activists, therefore, was the force of public opinion. This is what gained for them the attention of the press and the allegiance of the politicians.

The uprising of citizen protest demanding action to protect the environment demonstrates the reform potential in our democratic political system. As in other historic examples, such as sweatshop labor, adulterated foods, stock market manipulation, and the denial of civil rights, the environmental movement has shown once again that the public can successfully demand corrective action to redress patterns of social abuse. Yet citizens must understand that they have only themselves to look to when the public interest is being abridged. The glory of our system is that it does provide an opportunity for citizens to demand reform. The burden of that opportunity is that no one else will do the job for us.

Left alone, our government will not always look after the public interest. In the environmental area there is a natural, built-in imbalance. Private industry, driven by its own profit incentives to exploit and pollute our natural resources, uses its inherent advantages to exert political pressure to resist environmental requirements. The machinations of industry explain at least in part why the abuses of pollution became so severe before steps were taken to establish controls. It was not until conditions approached a point of horror that the public woke up to the need for reform.

Looking to the future, we must recognize that industry will continue to seize every opportunity to exert its political force. The question is whether those pressures will be counterbalanced by sustained assertion of the public interest. In this regard, we must look carefully at what has happened in the environmental movement in the years since 1972. One insight into this picture can be obtained by reviewing our efforts to resolve one of the most complicated and important of all environmental problems — the pollution that comes out of our automobiles.

PART III

The Challenge Ahead

CHAPTER 10

The Enigma of Clean Air and
Your Automobile

I HAD KNOWN Stan Benjamin for over two years and I should not have been surprised by his comment, but still it left me feeling deflated. Stan was the Associated Press reporter who regularly covered EPA, and he greeted every government announcement with suspicion. He and I were standing together beside a large round table covered with crackers, cheese, and bowls of dip at a reception held by EPA in December 1971 to celebrate the agency's first anniversary. "How do you think we're doing?" I asked Stan proudly. My mind was filled with all the progress we had made; I was not prepared for his indifference. "I guess you're doing OK so far," he answered, "but I'm still reserving judgment. I want to see how you handle the tough ones, like the auto suspension decision."

The auto decision was emerging as one of the biggest and the toughest we would have to make. It would ensnarl EPA in a conflict between public health and the public need to drive to work. The problem pitted EPA against the giant auto industry.

The fight against auto pollution runs back to the appearance of ugly Los Angeles smog shortly after World War II; to the controversies over how to control it, which raged in California throughout the 1950s; and to the imposition of the first regulatory controls on exhausts from new cars in California in 1966 and across the country in 1968. These controls did not solve the problem of smog; it continued to grow worse. Though the origins of smog are not completely understood, scientists seem to agree that its main component is hydrocarbons in auto exhaust. These are chiefly the result of incomplete combustion. The hydrocarbons themselves are invisible and harmless, but in sunlight they interact photochemically with other pollutants and with oxygen to form what is commonly known as "smog." The smog, of course, is visible. It causes eye irritation, aggravates asthma attacks, and at high concentrations may interfere with a person's normal respiratory and pulmonary functions. By the late 1960s smog was no longer a problem only in Los Angeles — it had invaded many other cities. Under stagnant air conditions, concentrations of smog built up to cover these cities with a thick, reddish brown haze so dense that it partially obscured the sunlight and left people coughing and rubbing their eyes.

National public protest brought the issue to a head in 1970 when Congress, prodded by a table-pounding Senator Muskie, enacted requirements in the Clean Air Act designed to end the problem once and for all. These required the auto industry to develop systems that would achieve a 90 percent reduction in the auto pollution allowed by existing levels of control and to install the new equipment on all new cars from 1975 on. The act pushed EPA into the middle of the problem by authorizing the Administrator to grant a one-year delay if the auto companies had made all "good faith" efforts to achieve that goal but had not yet developed the technology to do so.

The act provided that the auto companies could request the one-year delay any time after January 1, 1972. In March, Volvo broke the suspense and submitted its application for the delay, followed soon after by International Harvester, Chrysler, Ford, and General Motors. They were all to be covered by a single public hearing, and within sixty days Bill Ruckelshaus would have to make the big decision — to grant the delay or not to grant it.

Toward the start of the hearings, interest mounted both in and outside the agency. Special briefings were given to the press and to representatives of environmental groups. EPA's technical staff made a long and detailed presentation to Bill Ruckelshaus. That was when many of us got our first idea of the complexities of auto pollution control. We learned about the engine modifications most auto makers had already adopted to meet earlier pollution control requirements, and the new device that was to help them to meet the rigorous 1975 standards — the catalyst. Steve Miller, a young staff assistant, produced a crude, handmade model to explain how the catalysts work: as molecules of carbon monoxide or hydrocarbon pass through the minute openings of the device, a chemically active metal, which coats its surfaces, causes them to combine with oxygen, forming harmless carbon dioxide and water. Members of the technical staff from headquarters and from EPA's auto laboratory in Ann Arbor, Michigan, reviewed the most important questions. They described the masses of data received from each of the auto companies. We had also received a special report from the National Academy of Sciences; it had concluded that the technology was *not* available to meet the 1975 auto standards.

On Monday, April 10, public hearings opened in the auditorium at the Department of Commerce. A large group from EPA arrived early that morning and met in a small conference room to prepare for the session. Hardly anyone had been involved before in a proceeding like this, and the combination of its novelty and its importance made us all a bit nervous. I flipped through the pages of the thick documents before me and wondered if we would know enough to ask the right questions. A few minutes before ten o'clock everyone gathered up his stack of notebooks and papers, and we headed for the hearing room. It was not much different from a typical high school auditorium, with a raised stage at the front and a sloping floor with rows of several hundred theater seats. Most of the seats were filled, and the stage was bathed in the glare of floodlights. Two long tables were placed at angles to each other facing out toward the audience, one for the six-man EPA panel, the other for the witnesses. Several staff members and I slipped into the seats bunched behind the EPA panel. At ten o'clock Bill Ruckelshaus began to read his introductory statement, looking up into the television cameras. But within minutes the discussion became immersed in the technical issues.

The hearings schedule was jammed with a variety of witnesses — forty-four in all — selected to cover every side of the problem. First up was Volvo, the initial applicant, followed by others. As the hearings progressed, an atmosphere of relaxed though businesslike routine replaced the excitement of the opening minutes. The television lights disappeared at the luncheon break on the first day, returning periodically for expected highlights. Members of the press wandered in and out, only a few attending constantly. A few environmentalists also monitored the hearings, but the majority of observers represented auto manufacturers or other companies involved in the auto industry.

George Allen, EPA's top air pollution lawyer, who was presiding over the hearings, asked each auto company to describe its most promising system for emission control and to identify any problems it had encountered in developing that system. Led by those questions, the witnesses invariably talked about catalysts. None of the auto companies had made much progress in developing new power systems, such as steam or electric engines, and they had gone about as far as they could in making minor modifications to clean up the conventional internal combustion engine. The only real hope of achieving the statutory standards appeared to lie in the use of catalysts, but debate raged over whether they would work well enough to do the job.

It came as a surprise to me that the big auto companies

themselves were not attempting to develop catalysts. They were relying on smaller, independent companies to do the research and development work. The auto companies said that catalysts were plagued by problems. The catalyst companies replied that the problems had been solved. The auto makers said that catalysts might burn up or get overheated and thus become safety hazards, and Chrysler's Charles Hynan presented a melted-down hunk of metal as evidence. A representative of the New York City Police Department testified, however, that several cars equipped with catalysts had been used on police work for up to twenty thousand miles with no difficulties or complaints. Some witnesses claimed catalysts would be permanently poisoned by trace amounts of lead or other contaminants in gasoline; some said the catalysts would be shaken apart by an auto's vibrations. Test data to prove or disprove these claims were inconclusive. Much of the test data submitted by the auto companies failed to identify which model of catalyst had been used or why failures had occurred. There was a volley of arguments about the auto companies' lack of promptness in testing improved models as soon as the catalyst makers had developed them.

As the hearings weaved through the labyrinth of technical detail, there was gradually built up a mass of fact and opinion on the state of auto pollution technology and on efforts to improve it. Every scrap of information threw light on the tests laid down by the statute to determine whether a one-year suspension should be granted: Was the technology "available" to achieve the statutory standards for 1975 cars? And had "all good faith efforts" been made to develop it? Answers to those two questions would be difficult to obtain, but the ultimate decision to be made by Ruckelshaus would be even more complicated. A government official making a major decision must take the statutory standards and apply them to the facts, but that is not all he must do. His decision can affect jobs, health, and public attitudes. Bill Ruckelshaus had to consider the repercussions and subtle implications of what he was about to decide.

During the sixty days allowed EPA to act on the auto companies' applications, the process of making the decision moved forward at many levels. The chief arena, of course, was the hearings themselves, the most formal and most public part of the proceeding. Though they became enmeshed in detail, they retained their suspense — we heard that one witness for General Motors lost his breakfast before taking the stand. Other issues of broader consequence were considered informally behind the scenes. Through discussions at luncheon, in an automobile or in small meetings, Ruckelshaus and his top staff filtered information from personal conversations, newspaper accounts, legal memoranda, and a mixture of other sources. In the end, this task of harmonizing the details of a specific decision with his own sense of society's needs is an administrator's principal responsibility.

We had all gone into the hearings with the assumption that we would have to grant the suspension. After the technical briefings and the first few days of testimony, however, it became apparent that the auto companies were much closer to achieving the 1975 standards than we had supposed. At that point, we realized that we might deny the applications. The implications were scarcely comforting. Many people believed that the auto companies could not possibly meet the standards set for 1975 cars and that, unless relief was granted, they might even be forced to shut down production. Although we knew that the companies could reapply later for the one-year delay, they argued that they needed an immediate decision because of the long lead times required in their industry to gear up for production. Under these circumstances, denial of the requests for relief might be viewed as flirting with disaster for the nation's economy.

Our chief concern in this matter was with the White House — it was there that the most heated criticism would surely concentrate, both from industry and from other federal departments. As soon as the possibility of denial became serious, I urged Ruckelshaus to make contact with the White House staff so that we could explain our understanding of the problem. Ruckelshaus agreed, and I was dispatched to discuss the matter with John Whitaker one afternoon during the first week of the hearings.

John Whitaker's office was Room 100 of the Executive Office Building, one of the choice corner offices on the main floor. The room was spacious, attractive, and well furnished. Sunlight streamed through the windows, which offered a view of trees and green lawns stretching to the Ellipse and the Washington Monument beyond. As always, when I entered his office, I felt welcome and at ease. John Whitaker was warm, friendly, and approachable, a curious contrast to the stereotype of a hard-shelled political operator for which the Nixon White House became known. Yet Whitaker was one of Richard Nixon's oldest and most loyal supporters. He had worked for Nixon during his vice presidency in the 1950s, and during his campaign in California in 1962, and of course in 1968. John had even had made for his wife a pin containing two seals — one of the Vice President and one of the President — given to him by Richard Nixon a decade apart. Because of that loyalty, and because he was himself a geologist who usually favored development, Whitaker was viewed with distrust by many I regarded as close allies in the environmental cause. Yet friendships bridge issues, and I knew John Whitaker as a friend. We had worked together on many problems in the three years since we had met in 1969, and I knew that I could count on John's assistance and that he would always be honest to me.

At our first meeting I ran through the legal requirements, the technical problems, and the choices available for the

EPA decision, and stressed that we were seriously considering denying the applications. Whitaker listened intently and asked several questions, but he was not inclined to second-guess EPA's judgment on the technical issues. His concern focused on the effect our decision might have on the national economy. Would a decision to deny the applications cause unemployment? Would it disrupt the economy? I explained that we felt sure it would not cause such problems. It was not our purpose in that meeting to make any decision. We concluded by agreeing that I would keep in touch as the hearings progressed.

For two weeks it seemed that the decision might go either way. A turning point came in testimony presented one Wednesday morning during the third week by a young attorney for the Natural Resources Defense Council, David Hawkins. Hawkins had no technical knowledge, but his clear analysis established the perspective that controlled the final decision. He carefully pointed out the lack of firm evidence to support the contention that the 1975 standards could not be met, and emphasized several weaknesses in the assertions by the auto companies that they had made the all good faith efforts stipulated by statute. If EPA were to grant a suspension on the record that had been established, he argued, it would demolish the ability of the agency at any later time to insist that industry push itself harder to satisfy the pollution control requirements.

Ruckelshaus and I went out to lunch together after the morning's testimony ended. Still struggling with the decision as we ate our cheeseburgers and french fries, we reviewed once again all of the principal issues and the information we had on each. The encouraging results in a number of tests, the prospect that some recent improvements were not reflected in the test data, and the several soft spots in the auto companies' presentations concerning their development programs all supported a decision to deny the applications.

We finished eating, left the crowded restaurant, and wandered across the street into the small park at 13th and E streets, where we sat and talked for ten minutes more. Overhead a small bird hopping from branch to branch suddenly cut loose with its droppings, which hit Ruckelshaus right on the knee. With his usual good humor Bill picked up a leaf and started to scrape his pants leg, joking that this decision was proving a lot messier than he had expected. By the time we rode back to the office, I felt the decision was very nearly made, and Bill went off to get in touch with one of the most powerful figures in the Nixon Administration to enlist his endorsement for turning down the auto companies' request.

I returned the following morning to John Whitaker's office, where I went over recent developments and explained that we were now strongly inclined to deny the applications. Whitaker said that he would get back to me with White House comments as soon as possible. The chain of command above Whitaker was short and straight. Whitaker reported to John Ehrlichman. Ehrlichman reported to Nixon. That simplicity, however, was deceiving. From three years of dealing with the White House I knew that on any question of such major importance a variety of people could be expected to enter into the argument. Their identity and the positions each would take, however, were something I could only guess. The President had just left for Key Biscayne and would not be back until Monday. Whether the question would go to him would depend largely on the extent of the conflict in his staff. On Monday morning I received the crucial call from Whitaker: if we should decide to deny the applications, the White House would not object. My spirits soared — we had the go-ahead. The decision was not definite, but a critical phase had been successfully concluded and the field lay open ahead.

In the meantime the hearings had ended, and most of our

technical staff had gone back to the auto laboratory in Ann Arbor for the weekend to review all the data. They returned to brief Ruckelshaus on their analysis, which greatly strengthened the case for denial. Their conclusion was that the 1975 standards probably could be met by many models of cars, though not by all.

Now the burden fell squarely on George Allen. Ruckelshaus seemed 99 percent decided, but we did not want to disclose this fact for fear of a leak, which would have made his life hopelessly complicated if for any reason he might change his mind. Right away, however, we had to begin work on a written opinion to explain the decision, and Allen undertook to write it almost all by himself. On Saturday morning George Allen, Deputy Administrator Robert Fri, and I drove out to Ruckelshaus's home for a two-hour meeting, and Bill finally settled it — delay denied. Next hurdle: a press conference scheduled for Friday at four o'clock — after the stock exchanges would have closed for the day.

On Friday morning Ruckelshaus met with the EPA press people and other top staff to explain the decision to them. They greeted the news with delight. We then discussed how to go about giving advance notice to the most important Senators and Congressmen and to the auto companies themselves. Several press officers feared that the news would spread as soon as anyone was notified, but we could not avoid that risk. People with a vital interest in the matter deserved, and expected, to hear our decision directly from us. We agreed that copies of the decision would be distributed on Capitol Hill beginning no sooner than three-thirty. It fell to me to notify the companies, as close to the last minute as possible, and I made arrangements to reach senior executives of all five companies within the hour from two-thirty to three-thirty. I came back from lunch and began going down the list. I had wondered if they would argue with our decision, but each one received the news calmly and said he would want to read our explanation before making any comment. By keeping my eye on my watch as I made the calls, I managed to finish just in time to jump into a car and race across town to the new Federal Office Building, where the press conference was due to begin.

The large conference room was packed. As Ruckelshaus approached the podium jammed with microphones, I looked out at the members of the press — many familiar faces, many new ones — and wondered whether they were on to the decision. I remembered my conversation with Stan Benjamin six months earlier and wondered whether he would at last be impressed. The excitement of the long effort now building to its climax gripped me, and I could feel my heart pounding as Bill began to speak. He reviewed the statutory and technical background of the problem and referred to all the analyses made by the agency, including those aired in the exhaustive public hearings. He read on, almost skirting the decision, and then the moment was there: "My judgment, which is expressed in the decision which I am issuing today, is that these manufacturers have not established that present control technology is not available to meet the Act's requirement for 1975 cars."

Across the room, the tension broke. Someone in the back began applauding. With surprised expressions, the newsmen exchanged glances. Ruckelshaus kept reading: "I want to stress that the issue is a close one . . ." The opening statement was, of course, followed by a cannonade of questions. Although he had been nervous as he started to read the statement, Bill quickly regained his usual composure, and fielded the questions calmly, giving detailed responses.

The decision had an instantaneous effect on the employees of EPA. A sense of jubilation rippled through the ranks. Employees took the decision as confirmation of the agency's strength and integrity. I rode back from the press conference to EPA with three members of the staff and two young secretaries. It was like coming home after winning the big game. One of the secretaries put it simply: "I feel proud of our agency. I think we stood up to the auto companies and did what was right."

The decision demonstrated the Environmental Protection Agency's capacity to make an independent appraisal of the facts and not yield to the arguments of industry. The enormous stakes made this a test of the agency's stature. And the presence of the auto industry as the antagonist made the confrontation all the more dramatic. These factors enhanced the decision's popularity and gave it a far-reaching effect. The significance of EPA's strict handling of the auto industry was not lost on the rest of American business. On this account alone the auto decision was a significant event in the history of the environmental movement.

We had originally hoped the decision would be covered on the national news programs that evening, but when the press conference was scheduled for late Friday afternoon we thought that the opportunity was lost. What we had overlooked was that when big news breaks, the TV crews can really hustle. The announcement was fully covered on the evening newscasts. It was also widely reported on the front pages of the papers the following morning and was applauded in editorials around the country. Everywhere the decision was hailed as a victory for the environment and a triumph for the public welfare over the special interests of industry.

In the euphoria that followed the 1972 auto decision one might have thought that a solution to our auto pollution problems at long last had been achieved. Nearly everyone assumed that the auto makers could eliminate the pollution if only they were forced to do so. Now it seemed they would finally be compelled to do the job. The public clamor had resulted in tight statutory standards, which were being

strictly enforced. Optimism surely seemed in order. Unfortunately, the situation was not so simple, the solution not so
close. Subsequent events have told a sobering story.

Within EPA we knew that, despite our bold decision, the
auto companies had a long way to go before they could meet
the standards and that they also would have the right to
apply again later for the one-year delay. For the time being,
however, the issue disappeared from public view. The auto
company engineers went back to their research projects,
those involved in the hearings scattered to pursue other
interests, and the months began to tick by. The auto makers
filed suit in the United States Court of Appeals for judicial
review of the Ruckelshaus decision, and that case moved
slowly through litigation. On February 10, 1973, the court
overturned EPA's decision, stating in a lengthy opinion that
economic factors had to be given greater weight and that the
evidence did not justify a denial of the applications. The
court directed EPA to hold another public hearing. It was
about the time when the auto companies might have applied
again for the one-year suspension in any event, but the court
decision clearly strengthened their hands.

Hearings began anew. Once again we assembled a team for
weeks of intensive work. Once again masses of test data and
other information poured in for EPA's review. Once again
the EPA officials took their places at the hearing tables to
face succeeding waves of witnesses representing the auto
companies, catalysts makers, and others; and the auditorium
filled with observers from industry and with a few environmentalists. At this second set of hearings in March
1973, however, there were major differences. The testing
of emission control devices indicated that great advances
had been made in the past year; the improvements were
impressive.

At the hearings in April 1972 no auto company had
succeeded in running a car that met the 1975 standards for

the required fifty thousand miles, and very few cars had run as much as twenty thousand miles with encouraging test results. By March of 1973, however, several catalyst-equipped vehicles had actually been driven for the full fifty thousand miles and had met the standards through to the end. A number of technical problems had been conclusively solved. One welcome discovery was that catalysts would entail virtually no fuel penalty. In fact, by switching to catalysts instead of employing other techniques that reduced gasoline mileage, the auto companies would actually improve fuel efficiency at the same time they tightened pollution control.

It was clear, nevertheless, that the auto companies could not achieve the standards in the 1975 model cars. We had determined that the standards could be met, but not on a mass-production basis. Insufficient time remained to iron out all the wrinkles and to tool up for installing catalysts on all of the expected ten million 1975 cars. Ruckelshaus decided to grant the one-year suspension, though he tightened the requirements that had been applicable to 1973 and 1974 cars.

On April 11, 1973, Ruckelshaus announced his decision. It was to be one of his last important actions at EPA. Two weeks later he was transformed from a major figure on the environmental scene into a pawn in a far, far bigger chess game. President Nixon, flying back to Washington from a trip amid the rising tumult of the Watergate affair, phoned ahead from his airplane and summoned Ruckelshaus to meet him at the White House. Within hours came the public announcement that Bill Ruckelshaus had been appointed Acting Director of the FBI, replacing L. Patrick Gray, who had become personally implicated in Watergate misdoings. Ruckelshaus held the position for two months, and a short while later was appointed Deputy Attorney General. On October 20, 1973, his government service ended abruptly. When Elliot Richardson resigned rather than fire Watergate Special

Prosecutor Archibald Cox, Ruckelshaus was ordered to do so, and was fired by President Nixon when he refused.

The 1973 decision to grant the one-year delay was the first retreat from the strict statutory standards. Still bigger problems lay ahead. Most of the agency's research into health effects was carried out at Research Triangle Park, a huge campus-style scientific complex near Durham, North Carolina. A study was being conducted there by John Moran, whose name was about to become well known throughout the auto industry. Moran had been analyzing the effects of catalysts on the variety of additives and trace elements commonly found in gasoline. He concluded that although catalysts reduced hydrocarbons and carbon monoxide, they also caused higher levels of sulfates and other substances to be emitted from the tailpipe, with probable adverse effects on public health. While he was proceeding with this work, Moran explained his tentative conclusions to a reporter, whose news story caused a quick sensation.

The issue, which erupted in the first week after Ruckelshaus had left, landed in the lap of the Acting Administrator, Robert Fri. Stepping into command after two years as Deputy, Fri was stunned when he learned from the newspapers that one of EPA's own engineers was publicly questioning the catalyst, which we had recently endorsed. Moran's statements were immediately attacked by the EPA staff members in Ann Arbor and Washington, who had worked on the hearing decision. Personality conflicts became entangled with scientific uncertainties, and it took us some time to sort out the issues. EPA had foreseen that catalysts might cause unintended and harmful emissions — the question was to evaluate how serious the risks might be and then to balance them against the undoubted benefits of using catalysts to control the principal auto pollutants. After much internal wrangling, the agency reaffirmed its position in favor of catalysts, but many doubts remained. Though the fire was out for the moment, the ashes continued to smolder.

The auto pollution requirements then became the target for pot shots from another direction. If the auto companies, prodded by EPA, adopted widespread use of catalysts, this was bad news for the oil industry, which would be forced to remove lead from gasoline. A number of the big-name oil companies launched public attacks against the emission requirements, the most vivid, a series of full-page newspaper advertisements, sponsored by Mobil, headlined THE $66 BIL-LION MISTAKE. Mobil argued that the EPA standards were more stringent than was necessary to protect public health and would impose heavy financial costs for very little benefit.

Debate over auto emission controls intensified as EPA shifted attention to control of a different auto pollutant, oxides of nitrogen. For these too Congress had ordered a 90 percent reduction, but the deadlines were one year later. In June of 1973 we began a hearing on another request for a one-year delay. This request was granted, but again the requirements were made more taut than the previous levels of control. Our squeezing down on the nitrogen oxide controls made it more difficult for the auto makers to control hydrocarbons and carbon monoxide, and this made them complain all the more vociferously over the whole program of auto emission controls. In addition, the nitrogen oxide controls were expected to impose a substantial fuel penalty. The crowning blow was that evidence on the need for large reductions of nitrogen oxides was quite shaky, so even if all the problems were overcome, the public health benefits were uncertain.

It was against the backdrop of these difficulties that the energy crisis exploded in the fall of 1973. By then a full year's production of 1973 cars was on the road. They had been subject to far more stringent emission controls than earlier models, and the methods used for control had definitely hurt their gasoline mileage. As fuel shortages drove up the price of gasoline, car buyers made fuel economy one of the factors in their choices. New car dealers were stuck with large stocks of new 1974 models and found little market for the gas-guzzling big cars. The dealers howled in protest and started their own advertising campaigns. Concern over the impact of federal requirements on the auto industry continued into 1974 as the national economy began to slide into a serious recession. New car sales skidded, heading toward a slump that would result in layoffs of hundreds of thousands of auto industry employees.

The combined effect of these changes was to slow the momentum of the pressure to reduce auto emissions. Suddenly fuel economy, cost, and effects on employment emerged as factors to be balanced against pollution control in a way that was never envisioned in 1970 or 1972. Congress acted in 1974 to grant an additional year's delay before the strict statutory standards would take effect. It also authorized still another year of postponement to be granted by EPA, and after a public hearing in January 1975 the new Administrator, Russell Train, put off the strict requirements for the third time.

As a consequence of the three postponements, most cars produced for 1975, 1976, and 1977 are emitting or will emit roughly four times as much pollution per mile as the standards set by the 1970 Clean Air Act would have allowed. These higher emissions will continue as long as the cars remain on the road, well into the 1980s. Nor is this all. Congress immediately began to write further amendments, granting several years of additional delay before the strict standards will take effect.

The unraveling of the deadlines for achieving the stringent new car pollution control goals of the 1970 act is only part of the story. Another tale of frustration lies in the efforts to supplement those requirements by reducing auto use through the transportation control plans. The controversy and resistance ignited by those plans have hobbled any attempt to reduce the amount of auto use in the big cities with severe pollution problems. Unfortunately, the evidence makes it increasingly clear that if we follow our historic pattern of more people driving more cars more miles in the big metropolitan areas each year, many of our cities may never be rid of the afflictions caused by auto pollution.

In spite of these disappointments the federal new car program can boast of notable accomplishments. It tremendously intensified research and development, not only on catalysts but on many other systems of pollution control. The program has not achieved the result that some people hoped for, that of shifting the auto industry away from reliance on the internal combustion engine, but it has stimulated experimentation with alternative engine systems. It has also led to real progress in designing better carburetors, fuel injection systems, and other features to improve the performance of internal combustion engines. The program has resulted in steady progress in controlling auto exhausts. Although the ultimate statutory objectives of achieving exceedingly tight control still lie in the future, the interim standards represent enormous progress over earlier requirements. As cars meeting these standards are put into use, replacing older models, marked improvements in air quality in major cities can be expected.

One clear lesson from the country's experience with auto pollution is that when solution of a problem requires an advance in technology followed by widespread application of the new technology, progress will be neither easy nor quick. The development of effective pollution control systems for automobiles posed research and development problems requiring years to solve. Even then, ten more years will be needed to replace existing cars by new models with the best pollution control. To obtain the full benefits of the program, therefore, will require a timespan of fifteen to twenty years — a sobering fact that people seldom understand.

The whole experience must also make us think about the wisdom of relying solely on a technological solution to a problem of this sort. From the beginning almost the entire emphasis in the American effort to control auto pollution has focused on forcing Detroit to produce a cleaner car. For many people this has been a convenient approach. It supports the comforting notion that all the blame for auto pollution rested with those who produce the cars, not with the people who buy the cars and drive them. It also confirms the naive American faith in technology to solve every problem, without any sacrifice or adjustment in the pattern of people's daily lives. Yet the problems encountered in cleaning up the car suggest strongly that if Americans really want to end auto pollution in the big cities we are going to have to be willing to make some change in our unlimited dependence on the private automobile.

In retrospect, we can see that the events of 1973 and 1974 were of profound importance to national ambitions to eliminate auto pollution. In 1970 Congress made a commitment to wipe out the problem entirely. For the next two years the public, determined to achieve that goal, remained confident. Then a series of difficulties intruded. Slowly, subtly, without ever making a formal or conscious decision to abandon that goal, we altered our priorities. As the various obstacles arose and were accepted as being insurmountable, total victory over the bane of auto pollution quietly slipped beyond our reach.

The change in outlook on preventing pollution from new cars in a sense was symbolic of other events occurring throughout the national environmental effort. Beginning in 1973 conditions were turning adverse. Part of the reason for change lay in the inherent difficulty of achieving absolute goals of clean air and clean water. Part of it lay in the emergence of competing national needs. But perhaps the most significant part lay in shifting public attitudes. To see these changes in full perspective, we must look at the controversies then embroiling the environmental advocates.

CHAPTER 11

Pushing Too Hard?

I GLANCED AROUND THE ROOM in quiet dismay and thought to myself, "My Lord, what a difference." Half the seats were vacant, and I recognized many of the people present as employees of EPA. A number of others were representatives from industry, paid spectators gathering intelligence to flash out to corporate headquarters. At the most, I reflected, only a sprinkling of environmentalists had turned out for the occasion. A few observers were simply tourists who had wandered in to watch a congressional hearing in progress. Usually they left after ten or fifteen minutes.

The spaciousness of the high-ceilinged Senate Public Works Committee hearing room gave the proceedings an air of tranquil dignity. Bright daylight from the hot summer day outside streamed through the large windows along the left wall, making the artificial light superfluous. The minutes slipped silently by. At the front of the room, with his back to the audience, Russell Train sat alone at the witness table, answering questions in carefully phrased, well-modulated sentences, as he had done many times before. He faced a group of half a dozen Senators sitting behind the elevated semicircular wooden railing in chairs from which they could look out at him and across the audience. Several young staff assistants sat behind them. The questioning moved at a slow pace, each Senator waiting his turn to make comments and ask questions for a ten-minute period. It had been running for over an hour, and nothing had sparked excitement. Behind the Senators a trim-looking girl with flowing brown hair and a bright yellow dress walked across to the right of the room and came down the two steps to the press table, on which she placed a small stack of papers. A reporter looked up from the newspaper he was reading, distributed the copies around the table, and turned back to his paper. The confirmation hearings on the nomination of Russell Train to be the new Administrator of the Environmental Protection Agency were scarcely demanding his full-time attention.

The contrast between these hearings on August 1, 1973, and the Ruckelshaus confirmation hearings two and a half years before could not have been more striking. On the earlier occasion the hearing room had been jammed to overflowing, Senators seated at every chair, full television lights dousing the front of the room with brilliant illumination. Excitement had filled the chamber as people strained to hear every word. The contrast was in the questioning too. Ruckelshaus was cross-examined: Would he be strong enough to make the hard decisions required to achieve environmental objectives? He was challenged to fight for basic changes and to stop environmental abuse. In the hearings on Train's nomination hardly any Senator asked for assurance that the environmental values would be defended with sufficient vigor. The Senators' chief concern seemed to be that he not be too aggressive.

The hearings had been opened by the committee chairman, Jennings Randolph. He had held the reins over the committee during the upheavals of the environmental movement with unruffled civility and a touch of Southern charm, exerting a gentle moderating influence to guide the legislative forces but not to hold them back. Senator Randolph's opening statement had skillfully set the tone for the hearings. He had pointed out that the protection of public health is the foremost goal of environmental programs, but he had cau-

tioned that activities in this area must be balanced against
their impact on the economic strength of the country: "We
must not, in our eagerness to protect the environment,
become overzealous."

Senator Muskie had asked only a few questions and
excused himself to attend another meeting. Howard Baker of
Tennessee, the ranking Republican on the committee, was
deeply involved in the investigations of the Ervin Watergate
Committee and did not appear at all. Senator James Buckley,
Conservative from New York, asked whether Train's role in
implementing environmental legislation would be not only to
measure the environmental benefits but also to measure the
economic and social costs. The same theme ran through all
the other questions. Senator Quentin Burdick of North
Dakota urged that Train not oppose projects for irrigation
and flood control. Senator James McClure of Idaho, Senator
Lloyd Bentsen of Texas, and Senator Clifford Hansen of
Wyoming all voiced concern over the possible disruptive
effects of environmental requirements on the economic life
of the country and on people's standards of living.

In dealing with their wariness, Russ Train had several
personal advantages. Most of the Senators knew him well,
and they knew he was no young or starry-eyed extremist. His
background, his record, his temperament and manner, even
his looks, all reinforced the assurance that he would not
make hasty or reckless decisions. Russ Train was every inch
an establishment figure. In the capital's fast-paced political
and social life, Russ Train was a rarity — a person who had
not come to Washington but had grown up there. Son of a
Rear Admiral, he had gone to Princeton and the Columbia
Law School. After graduation in 1948, he had returned to
Washington to begin a career in government service. He
worked for several years on the congressional staffs of the
Joint Committee on Internal Revenue Taxation and the
House Ways and Means Committee; then, during the

Eisenhower years, he shifted to the Treasury Department. In 1957 he was appointed a judge on the U.S. Tax Court, and while serving in that job he became increasingly interested in conservation causes. He was the principal founder of the African Wildlife Leadership Foundation, and in 1965 he had resigned from the Tax Court to work full-time as head of the Conservation Foundation. Train had been tapped by President Nixon in 1969 to serve as Under Secretary of the Interior. A year later he was promoted to be the first Chairman of the Council on Environmental Quality, the job he held when picked to run EPA.

Throughout these years Russ Train's working days had been supplemented by evening activity in a city where the line between business and pleasure is frequently blurred. He and his wife lived in one of the city's finest residential sections, and moved quickly and easily into the active social life of the city's elite. At huge, jostling cocktail parties and small, intimate dinners, their circle of acquaintances steadily grew. It was no surprise that as Russ Train looked up at the group of Senators examining him he saw the faces of several men who knew him on a personal basis, who had been guests in his home.

Sitting halfway back in the audience, I watched Russ move effortlessly from one question to the next. A discordant note was injected, however, when the questioning passed to Senator William Scott of Virginia. Scott was a newcomer to the committee. He had been elected to the Senate just the previous fall, and was considered one of the most rigid conservatives in the Congress. A few minutes before he began to speak, a television cameraman had entered the room. As soon as the Senator started, the bright lights flicked on, and I felt the first pinpricks of apprehension at this quick change in the atmosphere.

Senator Scott announced promptly that he did not necessarily plan to vote in favor of confirmation. He expressed concern that enhancing the environment might affect the standard of living, and abruptly asked Train, "Would you advocate sterilizing all the people of the country, people who pollute?" He immediately acknowledged that his question was absurd but explained that he asked it simply to illustrate its absurdity.

Senator Scott turned next to the issue of using the taxing power of government to improve the environment. He asked if Train would approve of taxing a person who drives his car into the city. Boring in harder, the Senator asked whether EPA had the right to tell a person whether he could or could not drive his car. Vigorously he proclaimed his own belief that every person had a right to drive to work. Senator Scott then revealed that he had found Mr. Train listed in *Who's Who* as a "conservationist," and, while I listened in amazement, he cross-examined Russ as to whether he had approved that description and why he had resigned from the Tax Court to become head of the Conservation Foundation. Scott was suggesting that because Russ Train was so dedicated to environmental values he lacked the necessary objectivity to become the head of EPA.

Senator Scott's battery of questions was more than just the effort of a freshman Senator to reach for a bit of publicity. His opposition had a practical impact; the Senator exercised his privilege to delay the confirmation on the Senate floor until after the summer recess. That prevented Train from taking charge of EPA until mid-September. Worried by its possible implications, I marveled at the fact that the lone objection to Train's confirmation came from a man who disapproved of the nominee's describing himself in *Who's Who* as a conservationist. It signaled that public attitudes toward EPA had changed significantly. In the hearings Senator Scott introduced an article published that day in the *Christian Science Monitor*. It quoted various state and city officials who blasted EPA's plans to reduce auto use as "unrealistic . . . unworkable . . . ridiculous . . . suicidal!" Scott made his point sharply: "The cities and their representatives feel that we are pushing too hard at this time and that the people are not going to stand for it."

By 1973, environmentalism had lost much of its early glamour and henceforth would have to struggle for public support. Between the comprehensive statutes just enacted and the shifting forces of public opinion, the Environmental Protection Agency was about to be caught in the crunch.

The start of rough times for EPA had begun early that year with announcement of a proposal to curb auto pollution in Los Angeles. That was the city that had coined the term smog, where twenty years of hand-wringing, study, and protest had failed to control a problem, a problem that had, in fact, grown steadily worse. The Clean Air Act required the State of California to impose regulations to solve the auto pollution problem entirely not later than 1977. This posed staggering difficulties for state and local officials. The improvements in cars would be nowhere near sufficient to achieve compliance with the air quality standards by 1977 — that could be accomplished only by massive reductions in the use of automobiles, which raised the prospect of chaos in a city, famous for its sprawl, whose mass transit system had been abandoned many years before.

Faced by the apparent impossibility of meeting the statutory requirements, the officials had submitted a plan that was admittedly inadequate. Under the statute, the buck was now passed to EPA, and the municipalities of Riverside and San Bernardino promptly brought suit against EPA to force compliance with the federal law. This led to a court order directing EPA to propose, by January 15, 1973, a transportation control plan that would meet the statutory requirements. The court order raised blinding visions of a kamikaze mission, but it left no choice. EPA's analysis showed that solving the auto pollution problem by 1977 would require a

reduction of roughly 82 percent in the total number of
vehicle miles traveled during the heavy smog season, May to
October. The only way to achieve that was gasoline ration-
ing.

Bill Ruckelshaus unveiled the EPA proposal at a press
conference in Los Angeles. The public reaction throughout
the country was one of utter disbelief. It seemed incredible
that the Environmental Protection Agency could propose a
virtual shutdown of the auto transportation system in a major
United States city. The proposal would make it impossible for
people to get to work and would radically disrupt normal
living patterns. No one could believe that such a scheme was
in the public interest, however ugly the smog might be. To
the more knowledgeable observers, we succeeded in explaining that this plan had been forced on EPA by the
statutory terms of the Clean Air Act and the court order. To
most of the general public, however, the plan was simply
EPA's proposal.

On the morning before Ruckelshaus announced the proposal in Los Angeles, I was assigned to explain it to the
Senate Public Works Committee. The Congress elected in
1972 had convened the previous week, and five brand-new
United States Senators just assigned to the Public Works
Committee showed up for my briefing as their very first act
as members of the committee. We met in the large committee hearing room, which was crowded and noisy when we
entered. After members of my staff and I were introduced to
the new Senators, all of us sat informally around tables in the
center of the room, and I carefully explained the whole
background of the problem — the law, the suit, and the
proposal. As the story sank in, the Senators' eyes widened
with amazement. Their first impression of the controversial
environmental requirements could hardly have been more
jolting.

The Los Angeles proposal was only the first step down a

long and rocky path. Though smog in Los Angeles was more notorious than anywhere else, it had become acute in many other places. Our analysis showed that thirty-eight cities would require transportation control plans to reduce auto pollution. Due to the difficulty of developing these plans, EPA had allowed additional time to the state agencies to submit them. The Natural Resources Defense Council brought suit, however, and a federal court ordered the agency to promulgate these requirements. By June 15, EPA was ready to announce Transportation Control Plans for nineteen cities, including New York, Boston, Newark, Indianapolis, Pittsburgh, Philadelphia, Houston, Dallas, Minneapolis–St. Paul, and a revised plan for Los Angeles. The plans contained a variety of control techniques. They required gasoline stations to install sealing devices on gasoline tanks to prevent evaporation of fuel and also required periodic inspection of all registered cars to determine whether they needed tune-ups and other forms of maintenance. Many plans required changes in traffic patterns, such as the designation of one-way streets to reduce emissions by achieving a smoother flow of traffic. Other requirements called for exclusive bus and car-pool lanes to encourage car pools and use of public transportation. Most controversial of all were the requirements that discouraged the use of cars by restricting opportunities for parking or imposing parking surcharges.

The requirements posed a threat to every city. It was immediately clear that achieving the objectives of the Clean Air Act would require changes that touched citizens in their daily lives. The goals of public health — lessening the incidence of emphysema or heart disease — were in direct conflict with every commuter's immediate concern over how to get to work tomorrow. Acting Administrator Bob Fri laid out the issue clearly: "We are basically attacking the problem by asking people to change their habits — their long-standing and intimate relation to private automobiles. This is a fundamental change, but the only one that fundamentally will work." The impact was stunning.

Across the country banner headlines spread the news: U.S. ORDERS CAR CURBS TO CLEAN AIR — TOLL, PARKING BANS ARE SET FOR CITY, proclaimed the New York *Daily News;* AIR POLLUTION CONTROL WOULD LIMIT DRIVING, called out the Boston *Herald American;* "UNREASONABLE" CURBS FOR CLEAN AIR — Elizabeth [New Jersey] *Daily Journal;* YOU'LL PAY THROUGH THE NOSE FOR CLEAN AIR — Philadelphia *Daily News;* EPA CALLS FOR AN L.A. CAR BAN, N.J. GAS FREEZE — Chicago *Sun-Times;* AIR PLAN TOUGH ON CITIES — Kansas City *Star;* EPA ASKS AUTO BAN — Denver *Post.* The story was carried on page one of most daily newspapers, and coverage continued for several days. All reports emphasized the disruptive effect of the proposed plans. Two days after the announcement, the annual convention of the U.S. Conference of Mayors opened in San Francisco. The EPA Transportation Control Plans were the hottest topic in town, and outright hostility was the universal reaction. Even Bob Fri, in announcing the proposal, had acknowledged their extreme nature: "I am not sure," he commented in wry understatement, "these are the results that Congress intended." The sentiment was perhaps best captured by a simply phrased headline in the following week's *National Observer:* EMISSION IMPOSSIBLE.

Transportation Control Plans were not to be the only source of consternation as EPA carried out the Clean Air Act. Another explosive issue arose from a suit brought by the Sierra Club arguing that EPA had to impose controls to prevent any "significant deterioration" of air quality in rural or other regions where the air is purer than the standards would require. On June 11, 1973, the U.S. Supreme Court in a 4–4 tie vote affirmed a lower court decision in favor of the Sierra Club. The victorious Sierra Club insisted that rigid controls be laid down, and industry — especially the power industry — faced the prospect that large new plants might well be prohibited in undeveloped parts of the country. In response, the power industry and the United States Chamber of Commerce began a vigorous campaign to amend the Clean Air Act. As their representatives circulated through the power channels of the capital, spreading dire and exaggerated predictions of economic stagnation in all rural areas of the country, a movement got underway to effect changes in the law.

Something else was beginning to erode public support for the clean air program. There was a spreading concern over the effects of the auto emission standards on gasoline mileage. The standards had been tightened significantly for the 1973 model cars, and by the spring of 1973 word was out that the current models were giving a very poor showing on fuel economy. Stories circulated about cars that got only eight or even six miles to the gallon. The agency made an analysis of the 1973 cars and found that the emission control systems were causing roughly a 10 percent loss in gasoline mileage. It also found that many other auto features — especially automatic transmission, air conditioning, and, above all, sheer weight — combined to cause much more serious fuel penalties. But because of their novelty and the publicity given them, the emission controls bore the brunt of the blame for the poor performance. This was to remain one of the most widespread irritants eating away at the base of public support for environmental programs. It affected citizens in their daily routines in a way they could easily understand — and did not like. Complaints were especially strong in many rural areas not plagued by auto pollution, since the need for the controls in those areas was difficult to defend. No one, however, can tell when a car is manufactured in Detroit where it will be driven throughout the next ten years.

By the middle of 1973 a consensus was growing that certain amendments to the Clean Air Act would be required.

The heated controversies were also creating a situation in which relaxation of some statutory requirements was becoming politically feasible. This could be seen in a report by *Air and Water News* on the annual convention of the Air Pollution Control Association in late June. Its thesis was set forth in the opening paragraph: "If anyone has any doubt of Congress's readiness to make major changes in the 1970 Clean Air Act, that opinion was a well-kept secret last week. Most of those directly involved with air quality programs met in Chicago. Conversation — both off and on the record — started from one assumption: The Act will be modified. The only question is how."

In summer of 1973 a lull in progress could be observed across the entire environmental movement. More than the Clean Air Act was involved. The frenzy of activity before Congress adjourned at the end of 1972 had produced strict new laws to control water pollution, pesticide use, ocean dumping, and noise. With the turn of the year, environmentalists, fighting on a hundred fronts, had launched campaigns to address remaining objectives: land use, strip mining, toxic substances, and safe drinking water. By summertime the political power behind these drives had subtly, but decisively, softened. The fervor of protests by the general public against environmental abuse was less intense, partly because of the widespread belief that the biggest problems were finally being resolved. Attendance at public hearings had dropped off noticeably, and attention by the media slackened.

But in the work of the agency there was no letup. We had foreseen that achievement of the statutory goals of clean air or clean water would involve costs and burdens not fully appreciated when the laws had been passed. We had known that it would be our job to take the political heat of resistance to these requirements but to keep pushing ahead. And push ahead we did. The agency continued to establish the onerous Transportation Control Plans called for by the Clean Air Act and to carry out other stringent provisions of the environmental laws. At the same time we watched with mounting apprehension as the opposition to those statutes grew steadily stronger and more vocal. Yet we had no way of anticipating the challenge we were about to face.

By late summer spot shortages were occurring in a few specialty fuels, and energy experts were predicting a difficult winter ahead. A number of oil company advertisements began to appear in major newspapers, charging that environmental regulations were causing an energy shortage. Russ Train responded to these advertisements in his first appearance as EPA Administrator before the National Press Club: "There is a well-organized campaign afoot to propagandize the public into believing that our environmental concerns have been overstated and oversold and are the cause of major economic and energy problems," he complained. "This is hot air — pure and simple." For a short while the energy issue received relatively little attention; it was only one of many problems facing the environmental movement. Then in October the war began. In the Mideast it was a shooting war between Arabs and Israelis, and it quickly led to an event that America had never prepared for. The Arabs slapped an embargo on exports of oil.

Sudden fear gripped the country. People were afraid that there might not be enough fuel to keep homes and hospitals warm and factories running through the long winter ahead. In an atmosphere of national crisis, Congress moved swiftly to draft emergency legislation. By mid-November the Senate rushed through a strong bill to expand energy supply and curtail energy use. In the House the bill became the object of intense political tugging and hauling.

The energy crisis plunged the environmental movement into its most desperate struggle for public support. For the first time we were on the defensive, and a major rollback of environmental progress seemed imminent. The energy crisis handed a golden opportunity to our critics to attack the Clean Air Act. Environmentalists were blamed for having held back the Alaska pipeline, and Congress enacted legislation to permit immediate construction despite remaining environmental objections. The urgent need to expand energy supplies gave respectability to opponents of all the previously sacrosanct environmental requirements. As the crisis whipped up public anxieties over preserving the necessities of life, it added a raw political punch to claims that those requirements were excessively strict.

Conflicts between energy and the environment were played up constantly by the media. It was easy to state the problem as requiring a choice between satisfying energy needs and protecting the environment, and the natural tendency of the press to dramatize any conflict oversimplified and exaggerated the conflict between the two objectives. The energy crisis also had a more subtle effect in undermining support for environmental concerns. In seemingly every general newspaper or magazine the same reporters who had covered environmental issues were transferred to cover the fast-breaking action on the energy beat. Attention to the environment as a topic of national concern faded away, unnoticed by the general readership. Signaling this trend, *Time* magazine dropped its "Environment" section altogether in November 1973, after four years of regular coverage.

At EPA we saw the urgent need to expand the national energy supply, and decided to support moderate amendments of the Clean Air Act to allow full use of all available coal. We also recognized that some modification of the auto standards might be required to improve fuel economy. At the same time we launched an attack against the confusion created by the energy crisis. We hastily gathered the facts about the origin of the national energy shortage, and in

speech after speech pointed out that environmental safeguards had had little to do with creating the problem. We
emphasized that most EPA programs, such as pesticides
regulation or water pollution control, had no real impact on
the energy picture, and that there was no reason to slow
down our efforts in those areas.

Then at the height of the turbulence caused by the energy
crisis the Clean Air Act produced another bombshell. A
court order issued earlier in the year had required EPA to
establish restrictions over construction of projects that would
attract heavy auto traffic, such as shopping centers, sports
arenas, and large parking facilities. On October 30, 1973, the
agency published proposed regulations requiring government approval of such projects before construction began, to
assure they would not create air pollution problems. The hue
and cry provoked by this proposal was deafening. The
regulations were written to cover many projects that had
been in the planning for months and were about to go into
construction. To the builders and developers, the regulations
were a monkey wrench, thrown into their works at the last
minute, and they reacted with anger. The potential impact
on construction kicked up opposition from labor unions,
fearful of adverse effects on employment. Uncertainty over
the ground rules for evaluating air quality effects of the
projects added to the confusion and distrust. In Anaheim,
California, an emergency ad hoc committee from industry
and labor was formed to fight the EPA regulations. Their
fury was reflected in the local Orange County newspaper,
the *Register*, in a huge headline covering the top of the front
page: *Hard Hats Hit "Damn EPA."* Senator Barry Goldwater,
in a letter to President Nixon, expressed a bitterness felt by
many: "I resent it very much for some Washington, San
Francisco, or any other bureaucrat telling my state how to
run their affairs and ramming impractical and unreasonable
regulations down our throats."

All this turmoil provided Congress with the excuse, in drafting an Emergency Energy Act, to amend the Clean Air Act. There were provisions adopted by the Senate and House committees to grant power plants relief from air quality restrictions so that they could shift from oil to coal, and to allow industry a delay of up to two years in reaching the strict goals for reducing auto pollution. The rising antagonism against the auto standards was revealed more strikingly, however, by another proposal nearly adopted in a floor vote by the House of Representatives. Congressman Louis Wyman, a Republican from New Hampshire, proposed an amendment to permit the removal of all emission control devices from all cars, new and old. The EPA technical staff frantically tried to measure the dimensions of the disaster that would follow such a total abandonment of efforts to control auto pollution. The analysis showed that, due to the complexity of adjusting auto engines, the fuel economy resulting from such a change would be negligible. Congress, however, had little time for such technical considerations. The issue was hot, and emotions were ruling the day. The Wyman amendment was defeated, but only by the narrow margin of thirty-five votes.

Opposition to the Transportation Control Plans also peaked. Under the threat of even more extreme amendments than those adopted by the House, EPA reached a compromise agreement with the conference committee. Just before Congress went home for its Christmas recess, we agreed to eliminate all special charges on parking contained in the Transportation Control Plans, and we promised to postpone for one year any other restrictions on construction of new parking facilities. The irony was that these provisions were designed to reduce auto use. They would have cut down on the consumption of gasoline and helped to ease the energy shortage. Yet they became the victims of the panic and confusion that accompanied preparation of the emergency energy legislation. It was the first time that Congress had called for a step backward from any of the environmental requirements it had previously established. Fully aware that the struggle was by no means over, we looked ahead to the new year and wondered what it might bring.

Congress did not reconvene until the end of January 1974, and by then much of the furor had subsided. It appeared that the country would make it through the winter despite the oil embargo. Most people seemed to have accepted our contentions that the crisis could not be blamed on environmental regulations and that the country should continue its efforts to bring pollution under control. Proposals to add crippling amendments to the Clean Air Act encountered resistance in Congress, and as the months went by it became evident that even the changes so widely expected the previous summer would be very slow in coming. The basic framework of the environmental statutes had weathered the storm.

But a major change had occurred. During the spring of 1974 it became clear that opponents of environmental programs had attracted enough political support to be able to win on many issues. One example was the pending land-use legislation. Environmentalists had been pushing for years to establish a federal land-use program. They were heartened by the growing recognition that environmental protection can never be achieved until we develop better systems to manage our patterns of growth and development. Methods are needed to prevent indiscriminate development of marshes, scenic meadows, waterfront property, and other areas of special ecological importance; to curb runaway growth in sprawling metropolitan areas; and to guide the selection of sites for new industrial complexes. Environmentalists generally agreed that chief responsibility for planning and controlling land use should rest with state governments, not the federal government, but that a federal program was needed to establish basic requirements for the state programs and to give them the essential financial and technical support. A

strong bill to encourage land-use planning had been passed
by the Senate the previous year with broad support. A similar
bill was approved by the House Interior Committee, and
enactment of legislation seemed almost assured. Then, once
again, the unexpected occurred. With the evident approval
of President Nixon, the House Rules Committee voted
abruptly not to let the bill go to the House floor for approval.
Supporters of the bill were unable to recover from this
setback, and 1974 was to end without enactment of land-use
legislation.

The loss of momentum was clear with respect to other bills
as well. Strip-mining legislation, which had moved forward
strongly in 1973, drifted through most of 1974 and was not
passed by Congress until the very end of the year, only to be
vetoed by President Ford. Toxic substances legislation,
which had passed both the House and the Senate in 1973,
languished in conference committee through 1974 and died
at the end of the year. Even a popular bill to assure safe
drinking water met unexpected resistance because of concern over the costs of implementing such legislation and
objections to extending the federal authority. The bill was
finally enacted only after the highly publicized discovery of
hazardous chemicals in the drinking water supplies of New
Orleans and several other cities. The change in mood was
reflected by Congressman James Hastings of New York, who
was working on the drinking water supply act. "A year or two
ago if you described a bill like this as an environmental
necessity that would assure its passage," he commented.
"Now it's just the opposite, and the environmental label is
likely to attract more opposition than support."

As 1974 wore on we found ourselves confronting another
hurdle. The national economy was sliding into a recession
that was complicated by persistent inflation. Once more
critics pointed the finger of blame at the environmental
requirements, contending that the high costs of pollution

control were a major cause of inflation and a drag on economic growth. Once more we were in a race to get out information and to rally support. This time, however, the problem evolved slowly, without causing panic and without posing a dangerous threat to the basic environmental programs. National attitudes on environmental issues began to stabilize. *Time* magazine restored its "Environment" section. The results of the elections of November 1974 suggested strongly that environmental issues continued to attract broad public support.

The outcome of all the turmoil in 1973 and 1974 in some respects was a stand-off. Efforts to roll back the environmental programs launched earlier had achieved little. The country remained committed to controlling air and water pollution. On the other hand, the forward momentum of the environmental movement had been at least interrupted. The novelty of the movement had worn off, and the average citizen had become wary about the expense and inconvenience entailed in environmental reform.

The inversion in the political atmosphere remained throughout 1975. Legislative initiatives to deal with environmental problems were virtually nonexistent. The President sent no Environmental Message to Congress. Land-use legislation was briefly considered, quickly rejected, and abandoned for the rest of the year. Strip-mine legislation was again passed by Congress and again vetoed by the President; it too faded quietly away. Toxic substances legislation inched forward slowly. It was a year of little action to address remaining environmental problems or make new commitments to obtain environmental protection.

The record of the three years from 1973 through 1975 reveals that the environmental movement had entered a new phase, a phase best understood in reference to the dynamics of policy formation in our government. The year 1973 witnessed a dissolution of the national consensus that had supported demands for environmental reform. This was in part the result of the difficulties in carrying out the environmental programs already established and in part the consequence of the energy crisis. The situation was aggravated a year later by the recession. The inertia was also a result of the movement's success in helping obtain legislation to deal with several of the major environmental problems; that very success created the impression that public pressure was no longer needed.

The upshot was a marked decline in citizen activity to promote environmental causes. Public opinion polls continued to show public interest in environmental goals, but it could more accurately be defined as approval than as support. What was missing was the intensity that had characterized the activity of former years. At the local level citizen leaders were not mounting attacks on the remaining problems. The meetings and the mail fell off; every Congressman could feel the difference. And when the environmental movement lost the militancy of its grassroots leaders, it lost its political punch. At the same time, the political opponents were mobilizing their forces. The combination of these changes deprived the environmental leaders at the national level of the leverage they needed to achieve fundamental changes in national policy.

This profound change in basic political alignments had been recognized by Senator Muskie in his statement at the Train confirmation hearings in August 1973:

> Up to now those of us who are concerned with the environment have enjoyed a honeymoon period. It has been easy, relatively easy, to generate public support and congressional support for the goals that we have written into the law. Now we are getting into a crunch period and it is going to be difficult to maintain a balance and difficult to avoid the pressures of those who would throw away much of what has been accomplished . . .

Subsequent experience was to show that the environmental advocates were quite successful in resisting the pressures to throw away what had already been accomplished. Their problems lay in their loss of ability to move forward and resolve the many problems that remained.

CHAPTER 12

Piecemeal Progress

AT THE END OF MAY in 1971, I ventured out of Washington. In the scramble of the first six months at EPA I had scarcely left the city. Like many other high appointed officials who work feverishly but without firsthand knowledge, I had been laboring day and night to build a water pollution enforcement program but had never seen an "outfall." In fact, at the start I had never even heard the word, though it is the standard term for any pipe from which wastewater enters a waterway. The outfall is where the polluter bids good riddance to his wastes and they become a public worry. Murray Stein, serving as my mentor, decided to show me some outfalls.

We took three days and went to Buffalo, Cleveland, and Chicago. Our purpose was to explore the Buffalo River, the Cuyahoga, and the Calumet — rivers notoriously overloaded with industrial refuse, sewage, and filth. We began with the Buffalo, clambering aboard a Corps of Engineers ship early in the morning. We chugged slowly upstream, watching the docks, cranes, and warehouses of the waterfront glide by. Under a clouded, somber sky, the water appeared dull, deep, almost black, broken irregularly by the iridescent sheen from splotches of oil floating on the surface. We rode past huge plants that produce the steel, chemicals, and other basic materials on which our consumer society is based, and that also produce pollution.

Murray had invited a private citizen from Buffalo to join us on the trip, Stanley Spisiak, one of those impassioned volunteers Murray seemed to know all over the country. Spisiak kept up a running commentary about the Buffalo River. He mixed detailed information about the industries and their discharges with endless stories of his battles to dig out the facts on their pollution and bring them to public attention. Stanley Spisiak's avocation for over thirty years was building public pressure to clean up the river. For many years it had been a lonely battle, and the pollution got worse. Yet he had struggled on, sometimes receiving inside tips from employees of the polluters, passing information to local reporters, giving speeches to stir up other citizens. Finally his cause had gained support. He proudly pulled out an album of pictures, including one of Lyndon Johnson. As President, Johnson had also made a boat trip up the Buffalo with Stanley Spisiak. In the photograph the President is staring glumly into a bucket of slop that had been pulled out of the river.

Spisiak pointed out the outfalls, one after another. Many were under water but could be spotted by the bubbling or swirling disturbance of the water. Other outfalls stood brazenly above the surface. At some plants, concrete bulkheads were dotted with more than a dozen different pipes pouring separate streams of waste into the river. Spisiak told us that in many of those old plants nobody knew where all the pipes came from or even how many there were. At the Allied Chemical dye plant a large pipe poured forth a stream of deep red liquid, which splattered on the rocks ten or fifteen feet up from the water's edge. A smaller pipe nearby spewed out bright yellowish green wastewater. Our boat edged close to the shore and, as I leaned over the rail for a better look, Stanley Spisiak lifted his camera and clicked another picture — for his collection of "experts" he had educated on the problems of his river.

By occupation Stanley Spisiak was a jeweler, and before

we parted he gave me a small golden tiepin of a fish, symbol of life in the water. I put it on the green wool necktie I was wearing, where I have kept it ever since — a reminder that the power of the environmental movement comes from individuals, and that its leadership comes from any person who cares enough to search out the facts and insist that his protest be heard.

In those three days I saw more heavy industry — and more pollution — than I had seen in my entire life. In each city we took a boat trip up the river, and in Buffalo and Chicago we also made helicopter flights. I had been warned that I would be likely to pick up germs from such close exposure to the rivers, and by the time I came home my throat was sore with a mild infection. Yet despite the obvious filth, despite the prophylactics floating down the Calumet toward Lake Michigan, the marvel was that a few years before conditions had been even worse. Even I could see, for example, that enough progress had been made to ensure that the Cuyahoga would never again catch on fire.

Since I made that trip in 1971, things have looked up for Stanley Spisiak. In the spring of 1974 smallmouth bass and coho salmon reappeared in the Buffalo River for the first time in decades. Minnows and other small species of aquatic life also signaled the river's return to vitality. The long campaign against acids, oil, chemicals, and other poisonous industrial wastes at last was grasping at victory. Stanley Spisiak has now retired from his jewelry business to devote all his time to his environmental crusade, fully aware that the battle is by no means over. "I found that my job," he told me over the telephone in late 1975, "was interfering with what I wanted to do."

In the years since 1971 America has made genuine progress in tackling pollution, especially in our heavily industrialized regions, where the worst neglect had occurred. Efforts of the Stanley Spisiaks everywhere have produced results. Gradually, visible progress is being made.

Dramatic improvements have been made in Lake Erie, long thought "dead." The tireless struggle to reduce its pollution achieved a measure of success in 1974, when the Michigan Fish and Game Department felt sufficiently confident to stock the lake with twenty-five thousand brown trout, a species that cannot survive in polluted waters. In the same year over twenty species of marine life returned to the Miami River in Florida, once so polluted that nearly all aquatic life had disappeared. In 1975 a salmon was discovered in the Connecticut River, the first to appear there in decades. Many beaches that had been closed to swimming to safeguard public health have now been reopened. Some shellfish beds have also been restored to public use. Likewise, in the case of air pollution, it is evident that the air has become a bit cleaner in a great many cities.

Despite such achievements, the campaign to clean up pollution has suffered many setbacks. When public feeling against pollution hit its peak of intensity, political leaders set strict legal requirements to clean up the problems. But though they promised that the abuse would be ended within a few years, technical difficulties, high costs, and opposition from polluters placed roadblocks in the path. Buffeted by the constant controversy, the progress of the environmental movement has often seemed to be lost in uncertainty. The fact is that, though important progress has been made, major problems remain unsolved.

Auto pollution is one of the biggest. At this point it is unclear when, if ever, smog will be eliminated in a number of big cities. In several cities the only real hope lies in fundamental changes in systems of transportation, and at the rate we are moving it will take decades to realize that hope. Another intractable air pollution problem is presented by sulfur oxides. When the energy crisis of 1973 cut supplies of low sulfur oil and forced a return to full use of high sulfur coal, progress in reducing sulfur oxide pollution was disrupted. Installation of equipment to control this pollution has moved slowly because of its cost and the doubts that the equipment would be reliable. Many of the legal deadlines for controlling sulfur oxide emissions will be missed by several years.

One of the biggest disappointments in achieving statutory goals has been that the amount of work required has often been badly underestimated. Municipal sewage illustrates this clearly. The 1972 Water Pollution Act required that a high level of treatment be achieved by every city and town by 1977. At the time it was expected that the facilities for this treatment could be built for approximately $20 billion. In 1973 a new needs survey revealed that $60 billion would be required. The next year another survey was made; it concluded that $114 billion would be needed for those basic facilities, plus another $230 billion for other municipal sewage facilities provided for under the act. In addition to this expansion in the scope of work required, EPA experienced many delays in moving needed projects into construction. The net effect is that we will be nowhere near solution of the municipal sewage problem by 1977. Instead, we will still be building essential facilities well into the 1990s, by which time they may be outmoded. As of 1976 almost none of the sewage from Manhattan receives any treatment whatsoever — it is all dumped into the river raw!

The problems of auto pollution, sulfur oxides, and municipal sewage have been controversial and well publicized. A score of others have remained in the background, undiscussed in public debates but just as critical to ultimate success. An example is the problem of discharges by small industries into municipal sewage systems. All sorts of commercial and industrial plants are hooked up to municipal systems. Their wastes contain heavy metals, acids, oil and grease, chemical compounds, and other pollutants, but these diverse substances often cannot be treated by facilities designed to handle only normal municipal sewage. These pollutants, therefore, must be controlled where they originate, and the 1972 act added "pretreatment" requirements so that this would be done. Most cities, however, do not have any information on what is discharged into their labyrinthine sewer lines by the industrial plants, gasoline stations, and other business establishments hooked up to them. In addition, it will be extremely difficult to install effective treatment or control facilities on the site of old, small, and crowded industrial plants. On a nationwide basis these industrial dischargers account for a major part of all sewage dumped into municipal systems. Yet we have only begun the long job of cleaning up this pollution.

Another source of water pollution comes from surface water run-off. Rainwater trickling across mined areas — either strip mines or underground ones — picks up acid from exposed rock surfaces and carries that acid downhill. In thousands of miles of streams and rivers, especially in Appalachia, fish life has been wiped out by this acid drainage. The acid keeps flowing even after the mines have been abandoned, and often there is no one alive who can be blamed for the damage still occurring.

In agricultural areas, farm water run-off carries away silt, pesticides, and fertilizers, all of which damage the rivers and lakes downstream. In many regions such run-off is the dominant source of pollution, and until we learn how to prevent it no amount of industrial and municipal control will produce clean water. Yet there is virtually no national program now underway to bring a solution soon. A further complication is added by irrigation practices widespread throughout the West. The run-off of irrigation water bears heavy concentrations of dissolved salts, and as a large river moves downstream the accumulation of these dissolved salts can reach high levels. The Colorado River is now so salty that it is just about unusable for any purpose at the point where it enters Mexico. Again, no real solution is in prospect.

Similar problems afflict our national effort to control air pollution. Current strategies have focused on big industrial plants. In many places these efforts will reduce pollution enough to achieve the air quality standards. In other cases they will not. In the future, officials will have to impose more stringent controls on the big plants, chase down thousands of tiny sources (such as residential incinerators) to clamp some form of control on them, and grapple with the pollution that blows in from its origins several hundred miles away. In many of these cases we are only beginning to understand the dynamics of the problems we are urgently trying to solve.

On top of these obstacles to our basic pollution control programs, recent revelations have brought attention to bear on a new set of potentially frightening problems. These involve toxic substances, which can be present in the air or water in such minute amounts that they are difficult to detect.

One example is vinyl chloride.

In January 1974 the B. F. Goodrich Company announced the death of three long-time employees at its polyvinyl chloride plant in Louisville, Kentucky. The deaths had been caused by angiosarcoma, a rare type of liver cancer. Because of the rarity of the disease, the deaths aroused suspicions and touched off a search for facts. The weeks that followed rocked the chemicals industry. By June a total of thirteen cases of angiosarcoma occurring in men who had worked in the production of vinyl chloride had been documented. Government action followed swiftly to ban the use of vinyl chloride as a propellant in hairsprays, household pesticides, and related products. Emergency monitoring was conducted to determine levels of vinyl chloride concentrations in and around production facilities, and legal restrictions were tightened to cut the maximum allowable exposures in the plants. Medical studies on both mice and rats confirmed that vinyl chloride gas caused cancer, but it was unclear to what extent that risk pervaded the industry. As the base material for one of our most common plastics, vinyl chloride was being produced at a rate of seven billion pounds a year. It provided the foundation for a $12 billion industry employing sixty-five hundred workers and covering thousands of products, from phonograph records and toys to auto upholstery, floor tile, pipe, and flexible packaging. Only after the industry had grown to this size was its risk to health discovered.

The threat of cancer emerged in an equally unexpected way in the midst of a controversial water pollution case. Since 1955 the Reserve Mining Company has operated a mammoth iron ore processing plant in the town of Silver Bay, Minnesota, on the northern shore of Lake Superior. It dumps all its waste material directly into the lake — up to sixty-seven thousand *tons* per *day*. For years environmentalists, state agencies, and the federal government have attempted to force the company to stop those discharges. To support a law suit against the company, EPA collected data on the dispersal of the Reserve Mining pollutants throughout the lake. During the analysis an EPA scientist noticed that under the microscope the water appeared to contain minute fibers similar to asbestos. Experts who were called in later concluded that asbestos fibers, which can cause cancer, were present in the drinking water supply of Duluth. The Federal District Court ordered Reserve Mining to cease its operations immediately. The Court of Appeals reversed that order, however, and allowed the company to continue to operate, provided it agreed to shift to a system of on-land disposal of its wastes.

The fact that two courts disagreed on the handling of the Reserve Mining case is not a surprise. Neither decision offered an easy choice. Forcing the plant to shut down would have eliminated overnight more than three thousand jobs, virtually the entire working force in the town of Silver Bay. On the other hand, if Lake Superior, the largest freshwater lake in North America, is being filled with fibers that cause cancer, that is intolerable.

The Reserve Mining case points up the frustration of those who seek to protect our environment. After years of complaint, study, and litigation by the environmentalists, the company continues to operate, dumping all its waste material right into the lake. In keeping with our American tradition of freedom — born of the frontier and the woodchopper ethic — pollution is presumed innocent until proven guilty. On issues of scientific complexity, that rule places a heavy burden of proof on the environmentalist, though the risk to public health may continue until conclusive proof is presented. Even the discovery of a possible carcinogen did not shake the right of the polluter to continue operations.

Evidence of a link between environmental pollution and cancer has ominous implications. Next to heart disease, cancer is the biggest killer in the United States. It accounts for one sixth of all deaths, and its incidence is growing. Medical research has concentrated on detection and cure of cancer, rather than on prevention. Progress in developing medical relief has been important, but modest. Two thirds of all cancer victims die of it. The causes of cancer remain a mystery, but it is known that a person's chances of contracting the disease are increased by exposure to certain foreign substances that have been shown to be carcinogenic, and these may enter the body from food, water, and air. Our advanced industrialization now produces and distributes an unending variety of manmade chemical compounds. Many of these may cause cancer or other serious diseases. A good example is the pesticide dieldrin, whose use was suspended by EPA in 1974.

This pesticide had been used widely within the United States, particularly on corn in the Midwestern states. By 1973 residues of the chemical had been found in grocery surveys on more than 80 percent of all meat, fish, poultry, dairy products, and garden fruits. In March of 1974 the risks of dieldrin were graphically demonstrated when millions of chickens in Mississippi were found to be contaminated with the chemical at levels fifteen times more than allowable limits; the chickens had to be killed and buried. More disturbing was evidence revealing that over 99 percent of Americans tested had absorbed and retained residues of dieldrin in the fatty tissue of their bodies. Tests on mice and rats had been used to establish the carcinogenic properties of dieldrin. Out of curiosity, several of the EPA lawyers working on the case submitted their own blood samples for laboratory analysis; one of them discovered that his blood contained higher levels of dieldrin than those that had caused cancer in test animals.

The public has been almost numbed by successive reports of newly discovered health hazards. It is difficult to keep them in perspective, to realize that the evidence is still fragmentary and that many conclusions are merely speculative. Only as thorough studies are completed can definitive judgments be made on the severity of the risks. At this point we are just beginning to chip away at the evidence. In fact until the last few years we did not have much of the highly sophisticated instrumentation used to find and measure these contaminants, which in tiny amounts can threaten a person's life. In the meantime our dependence on chemicals, and our production of them, increases.

What we can see plainly now is our past ignorance. For decades we have used chemicals freely, without any thought to the dangers hidden within them. Mountainous volumes of chemicals have been distributed throughout the environment, and they will be there far into the future even if no more are added. But more are added every day. Our economy is dependent on chemicals — jobs, products, and profits — and so the production goes on. Traces of these manmade chemicals are everywhere — in the air, in the water, in our food, and in our blood and body tissue. They have been discovered in samples of human mothers' milk, and they have been found to cross the placenta and enter unborn infants. Some of these chemicals do serious harm to human health. Cancer is not the only danger. Chemicals can damage a person's central nervous system; cause brain damage; impair reproduction by causing sterility, still births, or birth defects; or cause a variety of diseases to a person's lungs, liver, kidneys, and other vital organs. Because of our general ignorance of which chemicals produce what results (and at what levels of exposure), we cannot quickly eliminate these risks. But certainly we must quickly resolve to eliminate our ignorance. Acceleration of scientific research and establishment of controls where risks are verified are both urgently needed. And we should realize that these problems will be with us for a long time to come.

In short, the battle against pollution is far from over. Both the obvious types of gross pollution and the subtle health risks only now being discovered defy immediate solution. The problems demonstrate the complexity of dealing with pollution. Passing a law does not by itself guarantee the achievement of results. A number of other preconditions must also exist. The pollution with which we now live is the product of years, decades, even generations, of neglect. What is required is a sustained national effort, with adequate funding, scientific research, regulatory power, and public support, to tackle severe problems one by one and stay with them until solutions are achieved.

The levels of pollution that remain today do not mean that efforts to save the environment have been a failure. They do mean that we have a long way to go before we can claim success. The growing number of outstanding cleanup achievements offers us encouragement. That sense of hope is reinforced by the construction, now underway, of many new facilities to control both air and water pollution; these should be completed within the next few years. The statutes passed by Congress have not achieved all their specific goals, but they have achieved their basic objective: to get this country moving toward better environmental protection.

More important than the first visible signs of actual improvement is the renewed strength of the national pollution control effort. The country is now on the attack with a mobilization of resources that offers real hope for ultimate success. This can be seen in the trend toward increased capital investment in pollution control facilities. Business and government spending have doubled, tripled, and quadrupled to billions of dollars per year. An entire new industry has sprung up: the manufacture of pollution control equipment. A notable expansion is occurring too in the development of monitoring systems, making it possible for the first time for interested organizations and government agencies to obtain detailed and reliable information about who is causing what pollution — the essential basis for insistence on control.

An important change has also occurred in the governmental regulatory programs at federal, state, and local levels. Many state agencies that were pitifully small and totally inadequate have grown in size and in effectiveness. Equipped with better staff, stronger legal authority, and more sophisticated information systems, these agencies are now able to handle pollution problems that are under their jurisdiction and require their control.

The critical need now is to maintain the impetus of the national effort against pollution. And that can be done only with strong, sustained public support. While many questions of the future will be technical, legal, or financial, the basic ones will be political. In many cases, new legislation will be called for. In others, renewed commitments will be necessary to achieve the initial objectives. As each issue comes to the point of decision within our democratic political process, one question will be asked again and again: Does the public still care strongly about the environmental concerns? Only if the drive of public concern retains its political power can we hope to achieve final success.

The shakiness of public support since we entered the crunch that began in 1973 makes it uncertain if the country will effectively confront many of the remaining big pollution problems. Campaigns to correct national problems of this sort tend to come in waves of public protest. At the peak of concern, that protest commanded attention from every public leader, and fundamental changes could be made. In the period of retrenchment, critics of environmental programs have strengthened their opposition, and the efforts of supporters have tapered off. Many of the regulatory programs will continue to be effective and to achieve important additional cleanups even with less public support. But additional changes must be made. Future questions will be decided by public opinion and by what individual citizens do at the grassroots level of political action.

Most people will not react to these issues on the basis of national statistics or surveys. To an individual citizen, concern with pollution is a personal matter. It grows out of his or her experience. It is likely that most people, applying their common sense, will conclude that it is far too soon to ease off on our environmental efforts. Unfortunately, despite the encouraging progress, conspicuous problems do remain. The most compelling of these are, as they always have been, the gross examples of pollution that are obvious — offensive to smell and ugly to see.

This struck me especially one day in the summer of 1974. Barbara and our children had gone to Maine for a two-week visit with friends, but our daughter Laura developed a persistent fever, and I had to drive one Saturday from Washington to Augusta to bring the family back. The day was clear, warm, and sunny, and as the miles clicked away I reveled in a solitude I rarely had in these hectic days. Passing through Maryland, Delaware, and southern New Jersey in the morning, I watched the countryside, fresh and green. Approaching northern New Jersey, I noticed that the landscape began to change, and the air did too. Amid quickening traffic, I entered the upper stretches of the New Jersey Turnpike — six lanes in each direction, each intersection a maze of bridges, ramps, and rushing, crisscrossing vehicles — and began to smell the odors of industry familiar to anyone who has traveled that road.

At the northern end of the turnpike one can look across to Manhattan, and on a clear day the tall buildings of the city's skyline stand forth impressively. On this day they did not. A dark haze hung heavily over the city, making even the buildings close to the highway appear fuzzy. Overhead the sun could be seen, but through the pall it cast almost no shadow. Unlike the white clouds of nature, this darkened mass of air came right down to ground level, confronting man on the very surface of the earth. I looked ahead at a large building whose outline I could barely make out, and began to watch my speedometer, counting off each tenth of a mile as I approached it. One, two, three, four, five, and I had passed it by. The haze of polluted air was so thick that it diminished the visibility of objects just half a mile away.

I marveled at the large new buildings under construction that I could see as I continued to drive through the immense metropolitan New York area — more buildings, with more smokestacks, to house more people, and more cars to bring them into the overcrowded, polluted city that is already America's leading example of mangled planning and over-developed chaos. I crossed the George Washington Bridge and whizzed through the underpasses and jumbled brick and concrete canyons of I–95 through the upper tip of Manhattan and the Bronx. With a sense of deep gratitude that I was not among them, I looked across the steel barriers at three lanes of cars backed up for more than two miles in bumper-to-bumper, stop-and-go traffic headed in the opposite direction. I followed the signs to New England with growing relief. The air lightened steadily as I drove east, and was sunny and bright by the time I reached Connecticut.

That personal encounter with pollution at the ground level reminded me of what I had seen in Pittsburgh three weeks before during a helicopter inspection trip. We had left the airport and headed through a mild haze toward the Clairton Works of U.S. Steel. From a distance the plant could be spotted easily by the columns of billowing black smoke rising from the ground. As we approached, the haze around us thickened until we were almost on top of the plant and had begun to circle it slowly. The U.S. Steel Clairton Works is a massive operation, one of the oldest and largest coke-producing facilities in the world. From the air it spread out beneath us in an intricate pattern of buildings, rail tracks, smokestacks, and other structures, its coke oven batteries laid out in parallel rows. Every few minutes a rail car would move into position alongside one of the ovens, and a gush of dark smoke would burst forth, momentarily obscuring our vision. As the smoke dispersed, we could see the rail car moving down the tracks toward a tall tower at one end, and then an even larger, though whiter, cloud suddenly enveloped the entire structure above it. Along the batteries of coke ovens we could spot several leaks, where small steady streams of deep reddish smoke were escaping. A large number of smokestacks of varying heights and sizes studded the whole plant, and a mixture of plumes of differing hues and intensities spiraled upward from them. A short distance above the ground the separate plumes and gushes of pollution blended and formed a band of haze that could be seen distinctly for miles and miles, until it finally dispersed into the mass of air overlying the region and mixed with pollutants from other sources.

We circled the plant five times, watching the operation and noticing different points from which the pollution was released. Each time the helicopter came toward the eastern side of the plant, we emerged into air that was almost clean, and then, as we completed a semicircle and came to the downwind side, we entered the heavy plume itself. It was so thick, we could scarcely imagine an operation more perfectly designed to create pollution. So overwhelming in fact was the air pollution that not until the fifth time around did I notice the dark outline of the water pollution being discharged into the Monongahela River from outfalls along the shore.

We left the U.S. Steel plant and moved downstream, passing over other steel facilities located along the river, their roofs covered with the deep reddish brown, slightly purple colors of soot from steel operations, each sending its mixture of plumes of dark smoke up into the sky. We passed the point where the Monongahela joins with the Allegheny to form the Ohio River, and followed its course downstream. The air, though still murky, lightened. Some twenty miles downstream we reached the Beaver River, which flows into the Ohio, and although the Ohio River had been brown and dirty all along, we realized at once that we had encountered a source of even more intense pollution. The outline of the darker waters from the Beaver could be seen far into the distance. Following the Beaver, we headed toward our destination, the Mahoning River, one of the most polluted streams in the country. That small river flows through the center of Youngstown, Ohio, and picks up an almost unbelievable burden of filth from its ancient steel plants. We saw two or three forks in the river before we reached Youngstown, and at each, the contrasting tones of color left no doubt as to the source of the pollution.

The evidence of pollution seemed out of place in the surrounding landscape. Except for a few scattered towns the countryside was rural, and the rich farmlands below stretched serenely in the golden sun as far as the eye could see. Even the Mahoning River looked lovely from the air as it meandered among the trees at its edge, though its color was almost dead black. When we approached Youngstown we once again spied the telltale plumes of smoke. Youngstown posed a special worry to us, since its steel mills were old plants with marginal profitability, and it was feared that the costs of controlling their pollution could shut them down. From the air it was clear that they were at the center of the life of the town and also that they were causing noxious conditions. We could plainly see the black murk of their discharges into the river, which was noticeably lighter and cleaner above each of the outfalls from the plants. The plumes from their smokestacks raised a cloud of dark pollution that cast a blanket of haze across the lands to the west.

Memories of that trip kept recurring as I drove toward Maine. Traffic on the Connecticut Turnpike was heavy. I flicked on the radio. It was the final climactic day of nationally broadcast proceedings in which the House Judiciary Committee was agonizingly drafting Articles of Impeachment against President Richard Nixon. I listened intently. Washington seemed far distant, and every minute took me another mile away. With a sense of remoteness, I wondered how long it would be before the nation recovered from the shock of that tragic episode.

My mind turned back from matters of national conscience to problems of national pollution. I thought again of the pall hanging over New York. I recalled my flight over Pittsburgh and Youngstown, and then thought of my visits to Buffalo, Cleveland, and Chicago and to other problem areas — Boston Harbor, southern Florida, the Houston Ship Channel, the Los Angeles basin. How long would it be, I wondered, before those problems would be solved? It would take a long while, longer, I knew, than most people ever dreamed, and as I had so many times before, I wondered how far the public effort would carry.

It was late afternoon by the time I approached Boston, where I stopped for a quick supper with my parents, and then headed north onto the Maine Turnpike as twilight descended. Shades of darkening pink replaced the blue of the sky, and slowly the sights along the roadside turned to silhouettes. Night had fallen when I passed Augusta and turned onto the winding, hilly, wooded country road that ran along the shores of Lake Cobbosseecontee. At last I parked my car in the still darkness by a small cove where my friend Erik Lund was waiting to take me across the lake to my family. As we pushed away from the shore, waves lapped at the side of the small boat. The air was cool and fresh, and the light breeze felt good against my face, sweeping away in a few moments the fatigue of hundreds of miles on the road. The stars above twinkled brightly. In the bare light I could see the dark form of the island directly before us as we moved across the lake.

Isn't it all strange? I thought. Some people live in the splendor of nature, fresh and undisturbed, while others are crowded in a jumble of buildings where even the sky above is darkened. What insidious inroads the wastes of our mechanized world make on the lives of people. Why would people not insist on cleaning up the filth and the ugliness? Why would they not be willing to make whatever effort it takes?

CHAPTER 13

The Squeeze of Scarcity

THE SUMMER AFTER that trip to Maine, Barbara and I took our children for a week's vacation to Windy Hill, just up the coast from Myrtle Beach, South Carolina. It was a spot we had been to before, a casual seaside community of simple wood frame houses that stretched out along the shore. We had rented the upstairs apartment of a two-story cottage with a view over the water. It was a delightful, unhurried place where we could play with the children, go swimming, read or play cards, relax, and unwind, with no telephone and no television, and only an occasional knock at the door that meant I must call my office.

We had gloried in the freedom of being out of doors and away from Washington. Laura and Nancy loved the beach, and Jack at six was eagerly learning to ride the waves. The first few days had seemed timeless, as though we would be there under the hot Carolina sun forever. Yet the clock was running. On Thursday morning we were out together walking. It was low tide, and the beach stretched into the distance, as far as the eye could see, with a width of more than a hundred yards of smooth, firm, clean, moist sand. A scattering of sunbathers dotted the upper stretch of beach in front of dunes covered by tall grass and sea oats, with the low-lying houses blending in behind them. The only noise was the steady crashing of the waves, rolling and breaking. Yet Barbara too must have felt that time was closing in upon us. I felt a tug of her hand against mine. "You know," she said, "it won't be many years more that we can come here and enjoy this beach as we've known it." I knew what she meant.

We had come to Myrtle Beach on our honeymoon, staying for one week at the sprawling and once elegant Ocean Forest Hotel. In the following years we had often returned, staying at a cottage with a more modest rental. Then one year we found that our favorite cottage had been sold and torn down. A six-story motel, complete with air conditioning and a freshwater pool, had been built in its place. Within a few years the adjoining lots were similarly transformed. It was nothing unusual, and like millions of others who have felt the effects of development, we made our own adjustment. Ten miles up the coast we discovered Windy Hill, and made it the site of our summer excursions.

That change had occurred in the 1960s, while I was still a lawyer in Boston, before we had become aware of an environmental crisis and before there was an EPA. Now I could read the signs more clearly and with a deeper sense of dismay. Behind us the skyline was punctuated by the outline of a new condominium. Down the shore we could see the outlines of other tall buildings in construction, one with a huge crane towering above — symbol of progress and an ever-rising gross national product. We knew of other lots closer by that had been sold and were awaiting highrise development. Enjoy every minute of it, I thought; your grandchildren won't be coming here.

The pressure of development along the Carolina coast is not a rare case. Rising affluence, faster transportation, and gigantic new earth-moving and construction equipment have made the development of waterfront property a booming industry. In fact, as our highway system stretches its web across the country, development is booming everywhere. The imprint of man's activities presses against natural scenic areas, wilderness, and wildlife habitat. The denaturalization of America proceeds unceasingly.

Even more distressing than this construction across the countryside is the intensive development in our metropolitan areas. More than two thirds of Americans now live in or around our cities. Land within these areas of dense population is subject to constant competition for industrial, residential, or other development. Every open parcel is vied for. A rapid climb in market value is usually combined with a real estate tax system that steadily raises the tariff on open land and an estate tax system that often forces development soon after an owner of open land dies. Few people can afford to keep land in an undeveloped condition merely to see a bit of foliage. The result is that huge regions where millions of people live have been deprived of areas of open space. In the Boston suburb where I played as a child, the fields and woods have now been replaced with houses. Children growing up in such places today will seldom experience the joy of running through an open meadow or of playing beside a brook. The lessons and the values of life in a natural setting are denied them. In their ignorance they may not even know what they are missing. And people *need* to enjoy the pleasures that come from exposure to nature!

These effects of economic growth and development crowd in on life in our world today. They represent the quiet cost of progress. They do not show up in accounts of the gross national product, except that each new investment would suggest that we ought to be enjoying a higher standard of living. The irony is that some of the advances actually erode the quality of human life. These side effects come partly from a lack of effective planning, but the problem is deeper than that. Growth and development are using up land that is in limited supply. It is not so much that we are running out of land; we are running out of the *best* land in the places where we need it most.

The pressures of development will only multiply. Growth feeds growth, and the bigger our economic base becomes, the faster it is able to expand. Our population is increasing and is concentrating into densely populated metropolitan zones. Our rate of consumption of electricity, minerals, and other raw materials continues to rise exponentially. Yet the base of natural resources to support all this activity is essentially constant. As a result, we are now facing new threats of scarcity — scarcity of land, of water, of air, of energy, of minerals, of timber, of food.

Pollution has seldom been seen as the depletion of natural resources, but it should be viewed in that light. The ability of a river to purify itself or of an air mass to cleanse itself makes each a basic natural resource. For decade after decade the volumes of our wastes have grown steadily, until the assimilative capacity of our streams and airsheds has become overburdened and exhausted. The stench of pollution is a warning that man's activities are overstepping the finite limits of our natural world.

Growing scarcities of other natural resources have repeated that warning. We have become dependent on foreign supply for many basic minerals, including over one third of our iron ore, over half of our zinc, silver, and gold, and over three quarters of our tin, mercury, and nickel. Shortages have occurred in paper and wood products, and commercial fisheries have been hurt by overfishing. Even supplies of water are pinching against our rising demands; quite aside from environmental objections, there is the fact we are simply running out of rivers we can dam. Most dramatic of all, however, has been the crisis in energy supply. More than any other single event, that shortage made it only too clear that our expanding industrial economy does depend on limited natural resources, and we are in danger that they might run out.

What has happened in this country is that we have used up

what were once vast untapped reserves. When the settlers first came here, the land stretched out before them with unbounded treasures of natural resources. It was, of course, largely those resources that brought the colonists here in the first place. Even then the European countries felt the need for new supplies of raw materials. The settlers found an abundance of timber, seafood, wildlife, and minerals spread across a majestic continent of virgin land, fresh water, and clean air. For over three centuries we have exploited those treasures. Without a second thought, we have gone from one source of supply to the next. As one mine is exhausted, another is opened. As one oil field is depleted, another is discovered. When one supply of water becomes inadequate, another river is dammed. If additional food is needed, more lands are put into cultivation. If more steel or aluminum or glass or concrete is required, additional plants are built. We have almost never confronted the possibility that new sources of supply might not be available for the asking. We are now, for the first time, posed with a disturbing question: How long will the finite resources of our earth meet our voracious demands, which are rising steadily each year?

These risks of resource scarcity have been the subject of incessant debate since the Club of Rome published its threatening report, *The Limits of Growth.* Experts have battled against experts. Some have warned that our economy is bound to collapse, pulling our civilization down in its ruins; others have assured us that our economy and GNP can continue to grow forever. But it is important for us to recognize that there is, of course, no way to test the validity of these predictions.

We cannot, for example, foretell future patterns of population growth or climatic conditions. Most of all, we cannot know what relief may come from technological progress. We can see that current energy supplies will run out, but we cannot tell whether new discoveries will save us from emergency. Or again, we can foresee shortages of minerals and agricultural products, but we do not know if substitutes will be found or new sources of food discovered. In summary, our current rates of growth cannot be sustained on the natural resources we know of, using the technology now available. That is a drastic change, which Americans must face up to.

Because of these uncertainties, the future may develop in any number of ways. The most probable course will be somewhere between the extremes predicted by the experts. Natural resource shortages are now so prevalent and severe, we cannot dismiss them lightly. Yet it may be possible to accommodate ourselves to future shortages if we exercise prudence and if we undertake concerted action. What is most likely is a series of shortage crises that will test our talents for adaptation.

From an environmental viewpoint, all these potential resource shortages are especially threatening. The energy crisis has already shown what can happen to environmental objectives under pressure of a resource shortage. After the Arab oil embargo, the immediate response by Congress was to set aside environmental impact statement requirements to permit construction of the Alaskan oil pipeline. Air quality requirements were relaxed to allow full use of coal. Auto emission standards were postponed to help cars obtain better mileage. And when badly needed legislation to regulate strip mining was finally enacted by Congress, it was vetoed twice by the President on the rationale, which was accepted by the House of Representatives, that America could not afford any restrictions on maximum coal production.

These examples illustrate that national policy decisions are often a matter of trade-offs. In an emergency, sacrifices sometimes are made. In any critical resource shortage, the environment will be at risk. Protection of the environment is but one part of a much bigger problem: managing the totality of our natural resources. We cannot permanently solve the environmental problems unless we can solve that bigger problem in its entirety.

In politics these problems become explosive when people's jobs are at stake. If resource shortages should cause a major disruption in our national economy, pressure would build for any needed sacrifice to get the economy running smoothly again. Environmental concerns could be trampled under quickly if, in such a crisis, they happen to be in the way.

Environmentalists, therefore, cannot wait until critical shortages occur and then attempt a defense against that pressure. By then it will be too late. To protect the environment it is essential that controls be established in advance to prevent such a crisis from occurring. The time is past when environmentalists can look only at specific concerns, such as water quality or wildlife habitat. Environmentalists must now address all aspects of the way in which our country uses its resources, whether shortages are likely to occur, and what will happen if and when they do. Prevention of disruptive resource shortages has a special importance to environmentalists, but it is a goal that all Americans share.

In actuality, environmental concerns over future economic growth have an extremely broad importance. The environmental objective is to assure that patterns of growth are planned and managed. The basic environmental rule is to look ahead. This requires conservation of scarce resources. This is just as important to a secure, vigorous economy as it is to clean air. The fundamental conflict is not between the environment and economic growth. The real question is whether we try to plan and control our future or allow unlimited industrial expansion to use up available resources. If sudden shortages occur, the first casualty will be the economy; risks to the environment are secondary. In the energy crisis, for example, several hundred thousand auto workers were thrown out of work when people suddenly stopped buying large automobiles, and similar layoffs took place in many other industries. Sound environmental planning, therefore, can also be the key to stable, beneficial economic growth.

To obtain this goal we all must turn to government. There is no other vehicle by which the public can carry out policies required to meet this public need. Competitive industry cannot establish safeguards against running out of supplies. So long as resources can be found, the free economy will gobble them up and price them at roughly what it costs to bring them to market. This is illustrated by the way we have exploited our domestic oil reserves, to the point that domestic production is now declining though consumption is still rising, leaving a gap that can be filled only by imports. If there is to be any restraint on consumption or development, it can come solely through government.

A place to begin is the use of land.

This is one case where we know we are confronting shortages. Continuous development is causing increasingly negative impacts on the surface of our land. Government action is required to guide future growth into patterns compatible with the long-term interests of people. Left unchecked, the market forces of private investment will inevitably find, and destroy, unique areas of ecological value that should be preserved for future generations; they will also compound the problems of overcrowded concentration in our metropolitan regions. The objectionable consequences of such development will get worse and worse until, as with pollution in the 1960s, the public demands that something be done. In many places the adverse effects of uncontrolled growth have created public and political obstacles to further growth. Local opposition has blocked new highways, airports, and power plants. In land use, therefore, sound environmental planning is becoming essential if there is to be additional growth. Some efforts to deal with these problems are now underway, but they are inadequate. Federal land-use legislation, along the lines of the bills developed and then dropped by Congress in 1974 and 1975, is imperative. It would provide funding, assistance, and direction to efforts at state and local levels, and efforts must be made at state and local levels to meet this urgent need.

The other chief area where government action will be required is more uncertain, but more momentous. It is the creation of systems to restrict or discourage consumption of specific resources — or even to ration them — if extreme shortages should develop. The most obvious area where this is needed now is energy consumption. An example of corrective action that has been taken is the 1975 federal law setting mandatory gasoline mileage standards to be met by the auto makers. This will force a degree of conservation, overriding the market pressures for larger, less efficient cars. Other stringent measures are also required. These should include new taxes on energy or energy-consuming products to encourage conservation. Not only must we adopt measures to reduce energy use; we must also try to foresee what other resources may grow scarce, and begin now to preserve our supplies.

In the face of these needs for government action, we must examine the ability of government to act. Our experience in environmental protection gives us a sobering warning. It tells us that we cannot count on government alone to solve our problems for us.

The most important lesson from our environmental experience is that government will not act to face hard national problems until the people demand that it do so. The government normally fails to see these problems coming, since nearly all top officials are preoccupied with the crises that have already arrived. But the real difficulty is that solutions to resource shortages will require wrenching changes in government policies (and private practices). This means that the key decisions on government policy will be subject to political pressure. This is inherent, unavoidable, and probably good — it is the essence of our democracy. But any restriction on the use of land or any other natural resource will surely encounter stiff opposition. Vested interests will send their lobbyists into action. Normally there will be no one to insist on such restrictions, even if they are, in the long run, in the public interest — no one, that is, until the public itself makes that demand directly and forcefully.

This means that effective government measures will not be taken to manage our use of resources until shortages are pressing against us. In fact, hard policy decisions are unlikely to be made until the problems are so acute that they are obvious to the average citizen. Only then will stringent measures become politically feasible. The whole complex process for establishing government policy must be kept in mind. Resistance to basic policy change can crop up anywhere in that system, and overwhelming political support is needed to overcome the weight of inertia. This delays quick response to problems, even after they have become clear to experts. It often prevents any strong action until they reach a stage of crisis. Then, when the people are near panic, immediate solutions are demanded. This, in essence, was the history of the government's response to pollution control.

The energy crisis also illustrates the failure of our government to grapple with hard problems until the pot is boiling over. By 1970 the experts knew that we were headed toward severe shortages of oil and natural gas. Yet nothing was done to head off those shortages. Not until the oil embargo did the government seriously address the issue. Even then little was done to achieve conservation of energy. Two years after the embargo, the United States was more dependent on foreign oil than it was in October 1973. Positive action seems to require imminent catastrophe. Then the people will lead, and the leaders will hurry to follow.

The only real alternative to waiting for a crisis to hit is

nationwide citizen leadership with enough foresight and political force to demand that these problems be faced before troubles arrive. This leadership should be drawn from environmentalists and from other concerned groups. It would require that individuals everywhere commit themselves to understanding the intricacies of these issues and then wage a campaign to educate the general public. Only if this citizen leadership comes forward shall we have any hope of meeting these challenges effectively. In both land use and energy consumption, we are already years too late.

The second somber lesson from our environmental experience is that even when the political pressures have developed so that policy decisions finally are made, years and years will still go by before government action produces substantial results. In its colossal size and strength the American nation is like a battleship moving at full speed. It creates overpowering momentum as it moves on any established course. No change in direction can be achieved by instant reflex. Whenever complex regulatory programs are involved, they raise legal, technical, and procedural problems that most citizens would never dream of. This is even more true if widespread capital investment, or basic research and development, or both are required.

In all the public debates over questions of the limits to growth, few people have focused on the ability of our government to respond to resource shortages. Yet that ability may be decisive. As our national economy continues to expand, threatening the finite resources on this earth, any one of many major problems may emerge as suddenly as our energy crisis did. Our ability to make essential adjustments can spell the difference between taking such problems in stride or suffering severe disruptions in our economy and our society.

The nature of our government is such that it does not anticipate problems; it operates by reaction after problems have occurred. But in many environmental and natural resource problems, government is our only hope. We can be grateful, at least, that government is responsive even though that responsiveness is dependent on demands by citizens to protect the public interest. For both those in government and those outside it, democracy requires a great amount of work.

To the person concerned with environmental values, the uncertainties we now face pose special dangers. The environmentalist, therefore, must have a special concern that our country anticipate resource shortages and prepare to meet them.

With the ever-increasing complexity of our world and our accelerating rates of resource consumption, this is an awesome challenge. Yet that is exactly the challenge we face.

Index

Index